Microsoft Windows Workflow Foundation 4.0 Cookbook

Over 70 recipes with hands-on, ready-to-implement
solutions for authoring workflows

Andrew Zhu

BIRMINGHAM - MUMBAI

Microsoft Windows Workflow Foundation 4.0 Cookbook

First published: September 2010

Production Reference: 1170910

Published by Packt Publishing Ltd.
32 Lincoln Road
Olton
Birmingham, B27 6PA, UK.

ISBN 978-1-849680-78-3

www.packtpub.com

Cover Image by Tina Negus (tina_manthorpe@sky.com)

Credits

Author
Andrew Zhu

Reviewers
Geert van Horrik
Ryan Vice

Acquisition Editor
Rashmi Phadnis

Development Editor
Dhwani Devater

Technical Editors
Gaurav Datar
Rukhsana Khambatta

Copy Editors
Janki Mathuria
Sanchari Mukherjee

Editorial Team Leader
Gagandeep Singh

Project Team Leader
Priya Mukherji

Project Coordinator
Leena Purkait

Indexer
Monica Ajmera Mehta

Proofreader
Chris Smith

Production Coordinator
Alwin Roy

Cover Work
Alwin Roy

About the Author

Andrew Zhu has six years of experience of software development and information technology: three years in Java, three years in .NET/C#. During these years, he designed and developed applications including computer language complier, SQL interpreter, Library book management application, online sale application based on JSF/Java, and SharePoint OA application. Two and half years ago he joined Microsoft. Since then, he has been helping developers solve IIS and BizTalk problems, developing .NET/Workflow/ ASP.NET/SharePoint applications for his customers. Now, he is a Technology Support Engineer working in Microsoft (Microsoft Globe Tech Support Center), Shanghai. He has been supporting WF4 since its beta1 version.

No book is the product of just the author—he just happens to be the one with his name on the cover.

A number of people contributed to this book, and it would take more space than I have to thank each one individually.

I must thank my colleague Steven Cheng and Packt acquisition editor Rashmi Phadnis—without you, I wouldn't have a chance to write this book. Thanks to Packt Development Editor Dhwani and Project coordinator Leena. You two stayed with me throughout the writing process. I cannot imagine what could come out without your help. Also thanks to Technical Editor, cool Gaurav and Rukhsana Khambatta. My thanks also go to the Copy Editor of this title Sanchari Mukherjee.

I want to thank the reviewers of the book: Ryan Vice, Dave Newton, Geert van Horrik, and Ryan Andrus. Thanks for your patience and comments. Without your effort, the book would have been full of mistakes and incomplete.

I also want to thank my colleagues from Microsoft: XianFeng Zhang, Guang Yang, SGuy Ge, Steve Danielson, Nate Talbert, and Dan Glick. Thanks for your help in the WF and WCF 4.0 discussion list.

Finally, I want to thank my Mom and Dad, thanks for your love and understanding.

About the Reviewers

Geert van Horrik, after finishing high school in 2001, decided he wanted to learn more about software development. During his education as a software engineer in university, he wrote a some applications using Delphi. Soon, he discovered the power of C++ and started writing open source projects.

During his study, one of his open source projects became very popular, and he spent most of his time writing new features for this project. After finishing education in Software Engineering cum laude, he decided to learn some more about business administration at another university. However, the combination of his addiction to software development and the open source projects made him quit the new study and start a company called CatenaLogic.

The most important product of CatenaLogic is Updater—a tool to easily deploy new versions of software on all clients. Geert van Horrik is also available as a freelance software developer, and mostly concentrates on the latest technologies such as C# and WPF.

Geert also loves helping other people with software development problems on forums, and tries to participate in open source projects in the spare time he has left.

Ryan Vice is an enterprise programmer with 10 years of experience working with Microsoft Enterprise solutions. Over those 10 years, he has worked on network security systems, high-volume e-commerce systems, title management systems, and a high-volume financial trading application. Additionally he has built workflow solutions for a geoseismic system and for a credit counseling management system. He has worked with both thick and thin clients and is currently specializing in the WinFX suite of tools. He was given Microsoft MVP in 2010 for connected systems and is an MSDN moderator. He also frequently teaches classes on WF throughout Texas.

I'd like to thank my father Ken for being a huge inspiration in both my career and my family, my mother Telsa for helping me get my career started, my beautiful wife Heather for all her support and love over the years and willingness to let me spend a lot of my free time tinkering with software technology, my daughter Grace for reminding me of how amazing the simple pleasures in life can be, and my new-born son Dylan for bringing so much more joy and love into our lives.

Foreword

Microsoft has been putting a lot of resources toward the development of Windows Workflow Foundation (WF). Therefore, before learning this new framework, it's important to understand why Microsoft feels it is so important. For WF 4.0, Microsoft went back to the drawing board and did a complete rewrite of WF technology with the goals of improving WF 3.5 by providing a WF framework that simplifies the development of workflow-based solutions and provides better performance. Microsoft's ultimate goal is to get a higher rate of adoption of WF and to attempt to make WF an essential component of the enterprise developer's tool kit. The questions that most developers and architects, who are first exposed to workflow, will be likely to have are:

- ▸ Why do I need it?
- ▸ Why does Microsoft feel it's so important to learn this new WF framework?
- ▸ What problems does WF make easier to solve to justify the non-trivial ramp up time for my team and me?

These are the questions that need to be answered before you start to learn the details of how to use the WF framework, as learning WF is not a small task and understanding the benefits would go a long way in helping motivate you and your team. This section of the book will help you better understand the "WHYs" of WF and lay the foundation for the rest of the book, which will allow you to hit the ground running by getting up to speed on the "HOWs" of WF. This book consists of short, easy-to-understand examples (or recipes) that show how to take advantage of the many benefits of WF. Your first read will allow you to get familiar with all the various features and extensibility points of the WF 4.0 framework and, as you implement WF 4.0 based solutions, you will find yourself coming back again and again to review these concise, easy-to-understand WF recipes. After reading this short book, you will be ready to simplify your enterprise development architectures by taking advantage of this powerful new workflow framework and all of its built-in, out-of-the-box features.

Let's get to it then... Why workflow? For starters, what kinds of problems does workflow make easier to solve? Let's suppose you need to build a solution for an accounting firm and that firm wants to have a system built to allow them to provide income tax services. This system needs to support the following features.

- **Account Creation**: The system will allow clients to create accounts either by coming into a branch where an employee can create the account via a thick client application or by allowing the client to create the account via a website.

- **Income Tax Information Submission**: The system will allow clients to submit income tax-related information for review by an accountant either in a branch office or on the Web.

- **Management of Assigning of Clients to Accountants**: The system will allow for the automated assigning of clients to accountants with support for manual updating of assignments.

- **Managing the Approval Process**: The system will allow for managing the review and approval process involved in preparing income tax papers for submission to the IRS, including management of requesting more information from clients, following up with clients, and routing information received from clients to correct accounts.

- **Notifications**: The system will allow for notifying clients of various account and tax submission-related events.

How would a system like this be built without using a workflow framework? Our first attempt might be to create a set of web services that support:

- Creating of a client account
- Submitting income tax information for an existing account
- Querying for income tax submissions assigned to an accountant
- Querying for a specific tax submission
- Requesting more information from the client about an income tax submission
- Approving the information submitted to indicate that the income tax information is complete and ready for an accountant to make an income tax return to be submitted to the IRS

This income tax process could take several weeks or months to complete and so it's not feasible that we could have a thread on the server waiting for the next input for an account to arrive. For this application to scale and work with any type of realistic enterprise volume, we'd have to persist the state of the account and when each web service request arrives, we'd have to take some kind of identifier (account ID or accountant ID) and retrieve the current state of the account before we could determine if the call could proceed. A client can't submit income tax information before they've created an account and the service for submitting income tax information would have to query our persistence store (database or whatever we are using) to verify this. All of this custom state-management code that would allow for sharing the account data among the various client applications from the various servers would need to be written by the developers including ways to deal with concurrency. We can't allow two clients to update the same data at the same time, so we'd have to provide for that in our implementation.

Assuming we get all that worked out, what about the parts of this process that aren't driven by web-services calls? How are we going to assign clients to accounts after they submit their tax forms? How are we going manage our notifications that will be sent to the clients when:

- We receive their information
- We approve or reject their information
- We need to request more information
- We've submitted their taxes to the IRS

We'd also need to build a scheduling system and an event routing (or messaging) system to help us satisfy these needs.

How do we deal with scalability? One solution would be to break apart the functional components of the application and deploy each one to a different server or set of servers so that you'd have a server for:

- Creating accounts
- Submitting tax data
- Assigning accountants to clients

Using this approach would allow us to scale but would make the application logic separated and hard to understand and maintain, as it would be spread over several deployments on different servers.

The ideal solution would be to have a framework that would allow us to:

- Build our workflow logic in a unified way
- Execute our workflow logic in a distributed way, across several servers

- Allow for easy sharing of and persisting of state without having to worry about concurrency
- Allow for easily creating events or messages that can drive business logic, including support for scheduling these events or messages
- Allow us to track the history of an account

If we had a framework that allowed for all these things, then it might be worth our time to go out and learn how to use that new workflow framework as it would provide us a lot of built-in benefits that would save us from having to reinvent the wheel over and over again. The good news is that this is only part of what Workflow Foundation provides. In addition to helping solve these problems, WF also provides:

- A re-hostable designer to allow us to create administration tools for visualizing and managing our workflow logic
- Support for parallel processing of tasks
- Support for creating our own workflow constructs (or activities) to allow us to model our own domain-specific languages
- An extensible architecture that allows us to provide our own implementations for things such as state persistence, workflow execution tracking, threading, and so on

Given all that WF 4.0 brings to the table, it's a worthwhile investment to learn this technology and add it to your enterprise development toolkit, and this book will help to get you up to speed in a very short amount of time.

Ryan Vice

MVP for Connected Systems

Table of Contents

Preface   **1**

Chapter 1: Workflow Program   **5**
Introduction   5
Creating the first WF program: HelloWorkflow   6
Creating a WF program using C# Code   9
Initializing a WF program using InArguments   11
Creating a WF program using OutArgument   15
Creating a WF program using InOutArgument   17
Using Variable in a WF program   20
Running a WF program asynchronously   22
Customizing a MyReadLine activity with Bookmark   25
Converting a WF program instance to XAML   29
Loading up a WF program from an XAML file   31
Testing a WF program with a unit test framework   34
Debugging a WF program   36

Chapter 2: Built-in Flow Control Activities   **41**
Introduction   41
Using the Foreach activity   42
A number guessing game in Sequence   47
A number guessing game using a flowchart   49
Using the InvokeMethod activity   52
Using the Switch<T> activity in Sequence workflow   63
Using the FlowSwitch<T> activity   67
Using the Parallel activity   69
Using the ParallelForEach<T> activity   71
Using the Pick activity   73
Handling errors   78

Chapter 3: Messaging and Transaction   81

Introduction   81
Creating a pure WCF service   82
Receiving and replying to a WCF message   87
Receiving and replying to a WCF message in code workflow   92
Sending and receiving a reply to a WCF message   98
Sending and receiving a reply to a WCF message in code workflow 104
Using CancellationScope activity   108
Performing a transaction by using TransactionScope activity   112
Performing compensation by using Compensable activity   117
Performing manual compensation by using Compensate activity   120
Performing confirmation by using Confirm activity   122

Chapter 4: Manipulating Collections   125

Introduction   125
Printing collection items   125
Using AddToCollection<T> activity   130
Using ClearCollection<T> activity   133
Using RemoveFromCollection<T> activity   137
Using ExistsInCollection<T> activity   141

Chapter 5: Custom Activities   145

Introduction   145
Creating an activity by inheriting the root activity   147
Creating a FileWriter activity   150
Creating a SendEmail activity   153
Creating an Input Message activity using Bookmark   156
Creating an Asynchronous HTTP Get activity   158
Creating a Composite activity   161
Creating an Activity Designer for the SendEmail activity   164
Creating an Activity Designer for the MySquence activity   170

Chapter 6: WF4 Extensions   175

Introduction   175
Configuring ETW tracking   175
Creating FileTrackingParticipant   180
Configuring the SQL persistence store   182
Loading a persisted workflow from the database   185
Using a persistence participant to persist additional data   189
Using a customized extension   195

Chapter 7: Hosting Workflow Applications — 199

Introduction — 199
Hosting a workflow service in IIS7 — 200
Hosting workflow in ASP.NET — 206
Hosting workflow in WPF — 212
Hosting workflow in a Windows Form — 216

Chapter 8: Custom Workflow Designer — 219

Introduction — 219
Implementing designer layout — 220
Implementing Toolbox, Workflow Designer, and Property Inspector views — 224
Implementing New Workflow and Load Workflow events — 227
Implementing Save and Save As events — 233
Implementing XAML Workflow Tab and Run events — 235
Implementing visual tracking — 238

Index — 247

Preface

WF4 is a process engine, as well as a visual program language, shipped along with Microsoft .NET Framework 4.0. Traditionally, when we design a long-running application, we break a large application into lots of small code blocks to address the business logic and use a database to store the intermediate data. With the growing complexity of logic, managing code blocks and authoring logic workflows becomes difficult. Now, with WF4, we can design and create distributed, long-running programs easily.

The aim of this book is to provide a step-by-step guide to help us start WF4 programming. Every recipe in this book is runnable.

What this book covers

Chapter 1, Workflow Program, provides recipes that will help us understand basic information about WF4 programming.

Chapter 2, Built-in Flow Control Activities, provides recipes that demonstrate the usage of the built-in control activities.

Chapter 3, Messaging and Transaction, provides recipes that demonstrate how to send and receive WCF messages in workflow. The second part of this chapter focuses on applying transactions in a workflow program.

Chapter 4, Manipulating Collections, demonstrates how to manipulate collection data in workflow programs with WF4 built-in activities.

Chapter 5, Custom Activities, demonstrates how to create our own custom activities; the most powerful unit of workflow.

Chapter 6, WF4 Extensions, demonstrates how to use the built-in extensions such as persistence and tracking, and also how to create our own extensions.

Chapter 7, Hosting Workflow Applications, mainly explains how to host workflow applications in IIS7. This chapter also provides recipes that demonstrate host workflow in ASP.NET, WPF, and Windows Forms.

Chapter 8, Custom Workflow Designer, helps us create our own WF4 workflow designer with visual tracking function.

What you need for this book

We need a PC having Windows Vista/7/2008/2008R2. We can also use Windows XP, but it is not recommended. .NET Framework 4.0 is a must. Once we install .NET Framework 4.0, we can run workflow applications. To develop WF4 workflow applications, we should also have Visual Studio 2010 installed on our computer. To host WF4 as a WCF service in IIS, we should install IIS7/7.5 in our computer.

Who this book is for

If you find yourself working with Windows Workflow Foundation 4.0 and you have basic knowledge of C#/.NET Framework/VB and workflow, this book is for you. It will be best if you know both C# and VB, because WF 4.0 expressions can be written only in VB (at the time of writing). With this book, you will be able to enhance your applications with flexible workflow capabilities using WF 4.0. To follow the recipes, you will need to be comfortable with .NET Framework, C# programming, and the basics of SOA and how to develop them.

Conventions

In this book, you will find a number of styles of text that distinguish between different kinds of information. Here are some examples of these styles, and an explanation of their meaning.

Code words in text are shown as follows: "The `ActivityLibrary` project is for all customized activities, whereas the `WorkflowConsoleApp` project is used for testing our customized activities".

A block of code will be set as follows:

```
class Program {
    static void Main(string[] args) {
        WorkflowInvoker.Invoke(GetCodeStyleWorkflow());
    }
}
```

Any command-line input or output is written as follows:

```
.NET Framework 4 Full (32-bit) - silent repair

%windir%\Microsoft.NET\Framework\v4.0.30319\SetupCache\Client\setup.exe /
repair /x86 /x64 /ia64 /parameterfolder Client /q /norestart
```

New terms and **important words** are shown in bold. Words that you see on the screen, in menus, or dialog boxes for example, appear in our text like this: "Click the **Invoke** button to get the result".

Warnings or important notes appear in a box like this.

Tips and tricks appear like this.

Reader feedback

Feedback from our readers is always welcome. Let us know what you think about this book— what you liked or may have disliked. Reader feedback is important for us to develop titles that you really get the most out of.

To send us general feedback, simply drop an e-mail to feedback@packtpub.com, and mention the book title in the subject of your message.

If there is a book that you need and would like to see us publish, please send us a note in the SUGGEST A TITLE form on www.packtpub.com or e-mail suggest@packtpub.com.

If there is a topic that you have expertise in, and you are interested in either writing or contributing to a book, see our author guide on www.packtpub.com/authors.

Customer support

Now that you are the proud owner of a Packt book, we have a number of things to help you to get the most from your purchase.

Downloading the example code for this book

You can download the example code files for all Packt books you have purchased from your account at http://www.PacktPub.com. If you purchased this book elsewhere, you can visit http://www.PacktPub.com/support and register to have the files e-mailed directly to you.

Errata

Although we have taken every care to ensure the accuracy of our content, mistakes do happen. If you find a mistake in one of our books—maybe a mistake in the text or the code—we would be grateful if you would report this to us. By doing so, you can save other readers from frustration and help us improve subsequent versions of this book. If you find any errata, please report them by visiting http://www.packtpub.com/support, selecting your book, clicking on the errata submission form link, and entering the details of your errata. Once your errata are verified, your submission will be accepted and the errata will be uploaded on our website, or added to any list of existing errata, under the Errata section of that title. Any existing errata can be viewed by selecting your title from http://www.packtpub.com/support.

Piracy

Piracy of copyright material on the Internet is an ongoing problem across all media. At Packt, we take the protection of our copyright and licenses very seriously. If you come across any illegal copies of our works, in any form, on the Internet, please provide us with the location address or website name immediately so that we can pursue a remedy.

Please contact us at copyright@packtpub.com with a link to the suspected pirated material.

We appreciate your help in protecting our authors, and our ability to bring you valuable content.

Questions

You can contact us at questions@packtpub.com if you are having a problem with any aspect of the book, and we will do our best to address it.

1
Workflow Program

In this chapter, we will cover:

- ▶ Creating the first WF program: HelloWorkflow
- ▶ Creating a WF program using C# code
- ▶ Initializing a WF program using InArguments
- ▶ Creating a WF program using OutArgument
- ▶ Creating a WF Program using InOutArgument
- ▶ Using Variable in a WF program
- ▶ Running a WF program asynchronously
- ▶ Customizing a MyReadLine activity with Bookmark
- ▶ Converting a WF program instance to XAML
- ▶ Loading up a WF program from an XAML file
- ▶ Testing a WF program with a unit test framework
- ▶ Debugging a WF program

Introduction

Considering workflow programs as imperative programs, we need to think of three fundamental things:

- ▶ How to define workflow programs
- ▶ How to build (compile) workflow programs
- ▶ How to execute workflow programs

In WF4, we can define a workflow in either managed .NET code or in XAML. There are two kinds of code workflow authoring styles:

- Creating a Custom Activity class
- Creating workflow dynamically in the runtime

There are also two ways to author workflow in XAML:

- By WF designer (recommended)
- Typing XML tags manually

Essentially, a workflow program is a .NET program, no matter how we create it.

After defining workflows, we can build workflow applications as we build normal .NET applications.

When it comes to workflow execution, we need to consider three basic things:

- How to flow data into and out of a workflow
- How to store temporary data when a workflow is executing
- How to manipulate data in a workflow

This chapter is going to focus on answering these questions.

Before moving ahead, make sure we have the following installed on our computer:

- Windows Vista/7 or Windows Server 2008
- Visual Studio 2010 and .NET framework 4.0

We can also use Windows XP; however, its usage is not recommended.

Creating the first WF program: HelloWorkflow

In this task we will create our first workflow to print "Hello Workflow" to the console application.

How to do it...

1. **Create a Workflow Console Application project**:

    After starting Visual Studio 2010, select **File | New Project**. A dialog is presented, as shown in the following screenshot. Under the Visual C# section, select **Workflow**, and choose **Workflow Console Application**. Name the project `HelloWorkflow`. Name the solution `Chapter01` and make sure to create a directory for the solution.

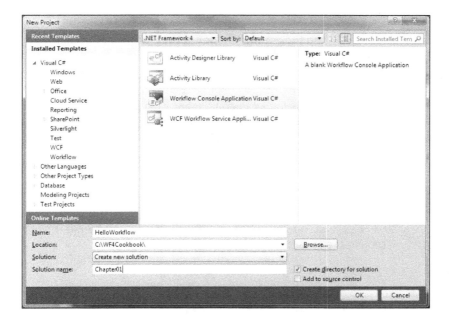

2. **Author the workflow program**:

    First, drag a `Sequence` activity to the designer from **Toolbox**, next drag a **WriteLine**
    activity into the **Sequence** activity. Finally, input **"Hello Workflow"** in the expression
    box of the `WriteLine` activity. We can see in the following screenshot:

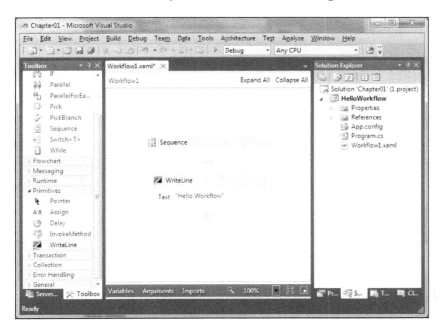

3. **Run it**:

Press *Ctrl+F5* to run the project without debugging. The result is as shown in the following screenshot:

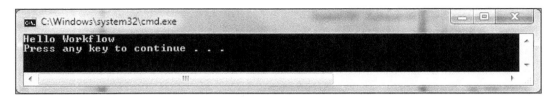

How it works...

When we press *Ctrl+F5,* Visual Studio saves the current project, and then it runs the project from the `Main` method in the `Program.cs` file.

```
WorkflowInvoker.Invoke(new Workflow1());
```

The preceding statement starts the workflow. After the workflow starts running, the `WriteLine` activity prints the "Hello Workflow" to the Console Application.

The workflow we created in WF Designer is actually an XML file. We can open `Workflow1.xaml` with an XML editor to check it.

 Right-click on `Workflow1.xaml` then click **Open With...**, and choose **XML Editor** to open `Workflow1.xaml` as an XML file.

All XAML files will be compiled to `.dll` or .exe files. That is why when we press *Ctrl+F5*, the program just runs like a normal C# program.

There's more...

So far, there are no officially published WF4 Designer add-ins for Visual Studio 2008. We need a copy of Visual Studio 2010 installed on our computer to use WF4 Designer, otherwise we can only create workflows by imperative code or by writing pure XAML files.

Creating a WF program using C# Code

In this task, we will create the same "HelloWorkflow" function workflow using pure C# code, beginning from a Console Application.

How to do it...

1. **Create a Console Application project:**

    Create a new **Console Application** project under the Chapter01 solution. Name the project HelloCodeWorkflow. The following screenshot shows the Console Application new project dialog:

    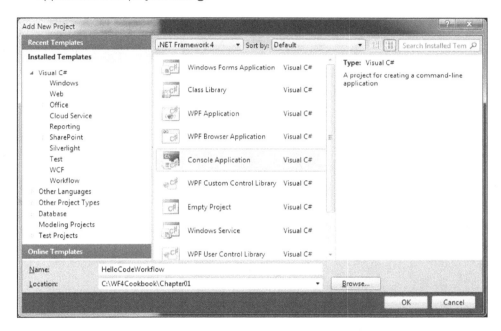

2. **Add reference to the** System.Activities **assembly:**

    By default, a new Console Application doesn't have reference to the System. Activities assembly, due to which we need to perform this step.

3. **Create workflow definition code**:

Open `Program.cs` file and change the code present as follows:

```
using System.Activities;
using System.Activities.Statements;

namespace HelloCodeWorkflow {
    class Program {
        static void Main(string[] args) {
            WorkflowInvoker.Invoke(new HelloWorkflow());
        }
    }

    public class HelloWorkflow:Activity {
        public HelloWorkflow() {
            this.Implementation = () => new Sequence {
                Activities = {
                    new WriteLine(){Text="Hello Workflow"}
                }
            };
        }
    }
}
```

4. **Run it**:

Set `HelloCodeWorkflow` as `StartUp` project and press *Ctrl+F5* to run it. As expected, the result should be just like the previous result shown.

How it works...

We use the following namespaces:

```
using System.Activities;
using System.Activities.Statements;
```

Because `WorflowInvoker` class belongs to `System.Activities` namespace. Sequence activity, `WriteLine` activity belongs to `System.Activities.Statements.` namespace.

```
public class HelloWorkflow:Activity {
    public HelloWorkflow() {
        this.Implementation = () => new Sequence {
            Activities = {
                new WriteLine(){Text="Hellow Workflow"}
            }
        };
    }
}
```

By implementing a class inherited from Activity, we define a workflow using imperative code.

```
WorkflowInvoker.Invoke(s);
```

This code statement loads a workflow instance up and runs it automatically. The `WorkflowInvoker.Invoke` method is synchronous and invokes the workflow on the same thread as the caller.

There's more

WF4 also provides us a class `DynamicActivity` by which we can create a workflow instance dynamically in the runtime. In other words, by using `DynamicActivity`, there is no need to define a workflow class before initializing a workflow instance. Here is some sample code:

```
public static DynamicActivity GetWF() {
    return new DynamicActivity() {
        Implementation = () => new Sequence() {
            Activities ={
                new WriteLine(){Text="Hello Workflow"}
            }
        }
    };
}
```

Initializing a WF program using InArguments

In this task, we will create a WF program that accepts arguments when initialized in the WF host. In WF4, we can use `InArguments` to define the way data flows into an activity.

How to do it...

1. **Create a workflow project**:

   Create a new Workflow Console Application under the `Chapter01` solution. Name the project `UseInArgument`.

2. **Author the WF program**:

Create a workflow as shown in the following screenshot:

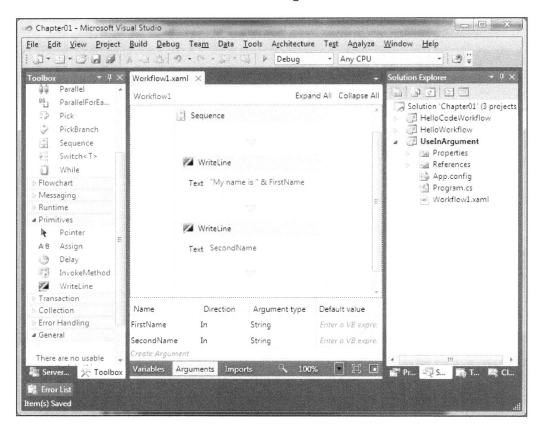

3. **Write code to host the workflow**.

Open the `Program.cs` file and change the host code as follows:

```
using System.Activities;
using System.Activities.Statements;

namespace UseInArgument {
class Program {
        static void Main(string[] args) {
            WorkflowInvoker.Invoke(new Workflow1()
            {
                FirstName="Andrew",
                SecondName="Zhu"
            });
        }
    }
}
```

4. **Run It:**

Set `UseInArgument` as **StartUp** project. Press *Ctrl+F5* to build and run the workflow without debugging. The application should run in a console window and print the following message:

How it works...

Consider the following statement from the code we saw in the preceding section:

```
FirstName="Andrew"
```

`FirstName` is an `InArgument` type, but how can we assign a string to `InArgument` without any explicit cast? This is because `InArgument` is declared with an attribute `System.ComponentModel.TypeConverterAttribute(System.Activities.XamlIntegration.InArgumentConverter)`. The class inheritance is shown in the following diagram:

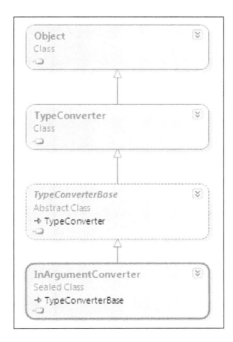

It is the `InArgumentConverter` that makes assigning a string to an `InArgument` possible. If we want to know more about `TypeConverter`, we can check MSDN the reference at `http://msdn.microsoft.com/en-us/library/system.componentmodel. typeconverter.aspx`.

There's more

In WF3/3.5, we can pass values to Workflow wrapped in a `Dictionary<T>` object. This also applies to WF4.

```
using System.Activities;
using System.Activities.Statements;
using System.Collections.Generic;

namespace UseInArgument {
    class Program {
        static void Main(string[] args) {
            IDictionary<string, object> inputDictionary =
                new Dictionary<string, object>()
            {
                {"FirstName","Andrew"},
                {"SecondName","Zhu"}
            };
            WorkflowInvoker.Invoke(new Workflow1(),
                                    inputDictionary);
        }
    }
}
```

If we are creating workflows using imperative code, we can use `InArgument` in the following way:

```
public class WorkflowInCode:Activity {
    public InArgument<string> FirstName { get; set; }
    public InArgument<string> SecondName { get; set; }
    public WorkflowInCode() {
        this.Implementation = () => new Sequence() {
            Activities = {
                new WriteLine(){
                    Text=new InArgument<string>(
                            activityContext=>"My name is "+FirstName.
Get(activityContext)
```

```
                    )
                },
                new WriteLine(){
                    Text=new InArgument<string>(
                            ActivityContext=>SecondName.
    Get(ActivityContext)
                    )
                }
            }
        };
    }
}
```

Creating a WF program using OutArgument

In this task, we will create a WF program that can return a result to the workflow host.

How to do it...

1. **Create a workflow project**:

   Create a new Workflow Console Application under the Chapter01 solution; name the project as UseOutArgument.

2. **Author a workflow**:

   Author the workflow shown in the following screenshot. Here are the detailed actions:

   i.   Drag a Sequence activity from **Toolbox** to the designer panel.

   ii. In the bottom of the designer panel, click the **Arguments** button, and click **Create Argument** to create an OutArgument string named OutMessage.

   iii. Drag two WriteLine activities from **Toolbox** into the Sequence activity and fill the textboxes with **"Start..."** and **"End"** respectively.

iv. Drag an `Assign` activity from **Toolbox** to the designer panel. Fill the right expression box with `OutArgument` as `OutMessage`, whereas fill the right expression box with the following string: **This is a message from workflow**.

3. **Write code to host the workflow**:

Open `Program.cs` file and change the host code as follows:

```
using System;
using System.Activities;
using System.Collections.Generic;

namespace UseOutArgument {
    class Program {
        static void Main(string[] args) {
            IDictionary<string,object> output=
                WorkflowInvoker.Invoke(new Workflow1());
            Console.WriteLine(output["OutMessage"]);
        }
    }
}
```

4. **Run it:**

   Set `UseOutArgument` as `Startup` project. Press *Ctrl+F5* to build and run the workflow without debugging. The application should run in a console window and print the message as shown in the next screenshot:

How it works...

Look at the following code snippet:

```
IDictionary<string,object> output=
    WorkflowInvoker.Invoke(new Workflow1());
Console.WriteLine(output["OutMessage"]);
```

`OutMessage` is the name of `OutArgument` we defined in `Workflow1.xaml`. the `WorkflowInvoder.Invoke` method will return a `IDictionary` type object.

There's more...

There is a third type of workflow argument: `InOutArgument`. It is a binding terminal that represents the flow of data into and out of an activity. In most cases, we can use `InOutArgument` instead of `InArgument` and `OutArgument`. But there are still some differences—for example, we cannot assign a string to `InOutArgument`, while it is allowed to assign a string to `InArgument` directly in the host program.

Creating a WF program using InOutArgument

In this task, we will create a WF program using `InOutArgument`. This type of argument is used to receive values and is also used to pass values out to the caller (WF host).

How to do it...

1. **Create a workflow project:**

   Create a new Workflow Console Application under the `Chapter01` solution and name the project as `UseInOutArgument`.

2. **Author a workflow**:

Create an `InOutArgument` type argument: `InOutMessage`. Author a WF program as shown in the following screenshot. In the **Assign** activity textbox, type **InOutMessage = "Now, I am an OutMessage"**.

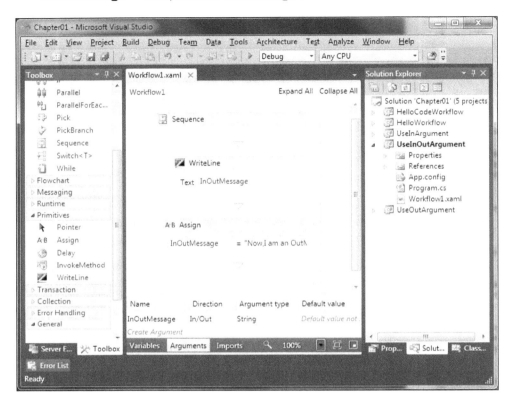

3. **Write code to host the workflow**:

Open the `Program.cs` file and alter the code as shown:

```
using System;
using System.Activities;
using System.Activities.Statements;
using System.Collections.Generic;

namespace UseInOutArgument{
    class Program{
        static void Main(string[] args){
            IDictionary<string, object> input =
                new Dictionary<string, object>()
                {
```

```
                    {"InOutMessage","Now, I am InMessage"}
                };
                IDictionary<string,object> output=
                    WorkflowInvoker.Invoke(new Workflow1(),input);
                Console.WriteLine(output["InOutMessage"]);
            }
        }
    }
```

4. **Run It**:

   Set `UseInOutArgument` as `Startup` project. Press *Ctrl+F5* to build and run the workflow without debugging. The application should run in a console window and print the message as shown in the following screenshot:

How it works...

The following code block initializes the `InArgument` value:

```
IDictionary<string, object> input =
            new Dictionary<string, object>()
        {
            {"InOutMessage","Now, I am InMessage"}
        };
```

This statement will run the workflow program with the input dictionary.

```
IDictionary<string,object> output=
            WorkflowInvoker.Invoke(new Workflow1(),input);
```

The string **Now, I am InMessage** is printed by the workflow. The string **Now, I am an OutMessage** is a message altered in the workflow and passed to the host and then printed by the host program.

There's more...

We cannot assign a string to `InOutArgument` directly, and the following style of parameter initialization is not allowed:

```
IDictionary<string, object> output =
    WorkflowInvoker.Invoke(new Workflow1()
    {
        InOutMessage="Now,I am InMessage"
    });
```

See Also

 ▸ *Creating a WF program using OutArgument*

 ▸ *Initializing a WF program using InArguments*

Using Variable in a WF program

We can use Variable temporarily to store a value when a WF program is running. In this task, we will create a WF program that prints five numbers to the console in a loop. We will use the `NumberCounter` variable as a number counter.

How to do it...

1. **Create a workflow project**:

    Create a new Workflow Console Application under the `Chapter01` solution and name the project as `UseVariable`.

2. **Author a workflow**:

    Add a `Sequence` activity, click the Sequence activity, create an `Int32` `NumberCounter` variable, and set its **Scope** to **Sequence**. Then, author the workflow as shown in the following screenshot. In the second **Assign** activity type **NumberCounter=NumberCounter+1**.

3. **Run it**:

    Set `UseVariable` as **Startup** project. Press *Ctrl+F5* to build and run the workflow without debugging. The application should run in a console window and print the following message:

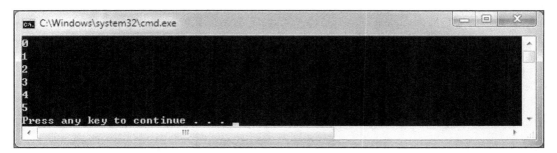

How it works...

To make the workflow logic easy to understand, translate the workflow into C# code. It will look like:

```
int NumberCounter = 0;
do
{
    Console.WriteLine(NumberCounter);
    NumberCounter++;
}while (NumberCounter <= 5);
```

While we can use arguments to flow data into and out of a workflow, we use Variable to store data in a workflow. Every variable has its scope, and can be accessed by activities within its scope. Variable in WF4 is pretty much like variables in imperative language such as C#.

There's more...

Please note that we cannot access to the workflow variables from the outside host. WF4 variables are designed for sharing data inside the workflow instance. We can use Bookmark to access the workflow from the outside host.

See Also

▶ *Customizing a MyReadLine activity with Bookmark*

Running a WF program asynchronously

In the previous tasks, we used the `WorkflowInvoker.Invoke` method to start a workflow instance on the same thread as the main program. It is easy to use; however, in most real applications, a workflow should run on an independent thread. In this task, we will use **WorkflowApplication** to run a workflow instance.

How to do it...

1. **Create a workflow project**:

   Create a new Workflow Console Application under the `Chapter01` solution and name the project as `UseWorkflowApplication`.

2. **Author a workflow**:

In the opening `Workflow1.xaml` designer, click on **Arguments**, create two `Int32` `InArguments` for **Number1** and **Number2**. Create an `Int32 OutArgument` for **Result**. Add an **Assign** activity to the workflow designer panel. In the **Assign** activity, type **Result=Number1+Number2**.

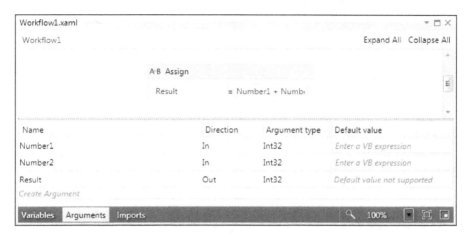

3. **Write code to host the workflow**:

Open `Program.cs` file and change code as follow:

```
using System;
using System.Activities;
using System.Activities.Statements;
using System.Threading;
using System.Collections.Generic;

namespace UseWorkflowApplication{
    class Program{
        static void Main(string[] args){
            AutoResetEvent syncEvent =
                new AutoResetEvent(false);
            IDictionary<string, object> input =
                new Dictionary<string, object>()
            {
                {"Number1",123},
                {"Number2",456}
            };
            IDictionary<string,object> output=null;
            WorkflowApplication wfApp =
                new WorkflowApplication(new Workflow1(),input);
            wfApp.Completed =
            delegate(WorkflowApplicationCompletedEventArgs e)
            {
```

```
                Console.WriteLine("Workflow thread id:"+
                        Thread.CurrentThread.ManagedThreadId);
                output = e.Outputs;
                syncEvent.Set();
            };
            wfApp.Run();
            syncEvent.WaitOne();
            Console.WriteLine(output["Result"].ToString());
            Console.WriteLine("Host thread  id:"+Thread.
    CurrentThread.ManagedThreadId);
        }
      }
    }
```

4. **Run it:**

   Set UseWorkflowApplication as Startup project. Press *Ctrl+F5* to build and run the workflow without debugging. The application should run in a console window and print the following message:

How it works...

The function of this workflow is adding two InArgument **Numbers** and assigning the result to an OutArgument **Result**.

```
AutoResetEvent syncEvent = new AutoResetEvent(false);
```

As the workflow thread runs simultaneously with the caller thread, the caller thread may terminate before the workflow thread. To prevent this unexpected program quit, we need to use AutoResetEvent to synchronize caller and workflow thread.

```
syncEvent.WaitOne();
```

The caller thread will wait there, until syncEvent is set.

```
wfApp.Completed =
delegate(WorkflowApplicationCompletedEventArgs e)
{
    output = e.Outputs;
    syncEvent.Set();
};
```

When the workflow completes, `syncEvent.Set()` is invoked. After that, the caller can continue running to its end.

Another thing we should be aware of is how we get the result when the workflow ends. Unlike the `WorkflowInvoker.Invoker` method, in a WorkflowApplication-style caller, we get dictionary output from `WorkflowApplicationCompletedEventArgs`'s `Outputs` property; see the preceding code snippet.

Customizing a MyReadLine activity with Bookmark

By using `InArgument`, `OutArgument`, and `InOutArgument`, we can flow data into the workflow when it starts and out of the workflow when it ends. But how can we pass data from the caller into the workflow when it is executing?—**Bookmark** will help us to do this. In this task, we will create a `MyReadLine` activity using a bookmark.

How to do it...

1. **Create a workflow project**:

   Create a new Workflow Console Application under the `Chapter01` solution and name the project as `UseBookmark`. Next, add a code file to this project and name the file as `MyReadLineActivity`. We can see this in the following screenshot:

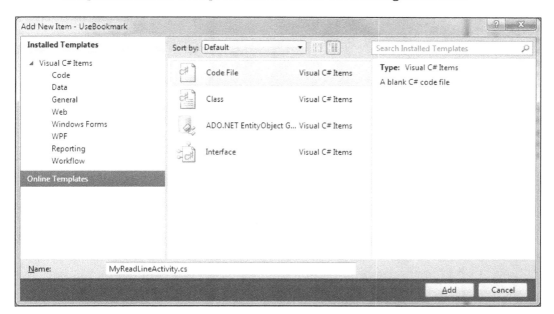

2. **Customize the activity with Bookmark**:

Fill the opening `MyReadLineActivity.cs` file with the following code:

```csharp
using System.Activities;
namespace UseBookmark{
    public class MyReadLine : NativeActivity<string>{
        [RequiredArgument]
        public InArgument<string> BookmarkName { get; set; }
        protected override void Execute(
            NativeActivityContext context)
        {
            context.CreateBookmark(BookmarkName.Get(context),
                    new BookmarkCallback(OnResumeBookmark));
        }
        protected override bool CanInduceIdle
        {
            get
            {
                { return true;}
            }
        }
        public void OnResumeBookmark(
            NativeActivityContext context,
            Bookmark bookmark,
            object obj)
        {
            Result.Set(context, (string)obj);
        }
    }
}
```

Save the file and press *F6* to build the project so that the activity will appear in the WF designer activity toolbox.

3. **Author a workflow**:

Open `Workflow1.xaml` and author the workflow as shown in the following screenshot:

4. **Write code to host the workflow**:

Open `Program.cs` file and change the code as follows:

```
using System;
using System.Linq;
using System.Activities;
using System.Activities.Statements;
using System.Threading;

namespace UseBookmark{
    class Program{
```

```
static void Main(string[] args)
{
    AutoResetEvent syncEvent =
        new AutoResetEvent(false);
    string bookmarkName="GreetingBookmark";
    WorkflowApplication wfApp =
        new WorkflowApplication(new Workflow1()
    {
        BookmarkNameInArg=bookmarkName
    });
    wfApp.Completed = delegate(
        WorkflowApplicationCompletedEventArgs e)
    {
        syncEvent.Set();
    };
    wfApp.Run();
    wfApp.ResumeBookmark(bookmarkName,
        Console.ReadLine());
    syncEvent.WaitOne();
}
}
}
```

5. **Run it**:

   Set UseBookmark as Startup project. Press *Ctrl+F5* to build and run the workflow without debugging. The application should run in a console window and print the message as shown in the following screenshot:

How it works...

In the code shown in the second step, we create a class inherited from NativeActivity. NativeActivity is a special abstract activity that can be used to customize complex activities; we will talk about it more in *Chapter 5, Custom Activities*.

```
context.CreateBookmark(BookmarkName.Get(context),
        new BookmarkCallback(OnResumeBookmark));
```

By this statement, the WF context creates a Bookmark with arguments `BookMarkName` and `BookMarkCallback`. When the `wfApp.ResumeBookmark` method is called, the `OnResumeBookmark` that was defined in the Customized Activity body will be executed.

```
protected override bool CanInduceIdle{
    get
    {
        { return true; }
    }
}
```

This is a built-in property that indicates whether the customized activity can cause the workflow to become idle; the default value is `false`.

Consider the following code snippet of step 3:

```
wfApp.ResumeBookmark(bookmarkName,
                Console.ReadLine());
```

When this statement is executed, the `OnResumeBookmark` method defined in the `MyReadLine` activity will be called and the method will accept the value passed via `Console.ReadLine()`.

Converting a WF program instance to XAML

In real applications, we would like to write and test WF programs in imperative code, while storing, running, and transmitting workflow as an XAML string or file. In this task, we will convert a WF program instance to an XAML string.

How to do it...

1. **Create a workflow project**:

   Create a new **Workflow Console Application** under the `Chapter01` solution and name the project `ConvertWFInstanceToXML`. Delete the `Workflow1.xaml` file that is created by default.

2. **Write code to create the workflow and its host**:

   Open `Program.cs` file and change the code as follows:

```
using System;
using System.Activities;
using System.Activities.Statements;
using System.Text;
using System.Xaml;
using System.Activities.XamlIntegration;
```

```
using System.IO;

namespace ConvertWFObjectToXML {
    class Program {
        static void Main(string[] args) {
            //Create a Workflow instance object
ActivityBuilder ab = new ActivityBuilder();
            ab.Implementation = new Sequence()
            {
                Activities =
                {
                    new WriteLine{Text="Message from Workflow"}
                }
            };

            //Convert Workflow instance to xml string
            StringBuilder sb = new StringBuilder();
            StringWriter sw = new StringWriter(sb);
            XamlWriter xw =
                ActivityXamlServices.CreateBuilderWriter(
                new XamlXmlWriter(sw,
                                new XamlSchemaContext()));
            XamlServices.Save(xw, ab);
            Console.WriteLine(sb.ToString());
        }
    }
}
```

3. **Run it**:

   Set `ConvertWFInstanceToXML` as **Startup** project. Press *Ctrl+F5* to build and run the workflow without debugging. The application should run in a console window and print the message as shown in the following screenshot:

Consider the following XML string reformatted from the screenshot:

```
<?xml version="1.0" encoding="utf-16"?>
<Activity  x:Class="{x:Null}"
                xmlns="http://schemas.microsoft.com/netfx/2009/
xaml/activities"
                xmlns:x="http://schemas.microsoft.com/
winfx/2006/xaml">
     <Sequence>
          <WriteLine Text="Hello" />
     </Sequence>
</Activity>
```

How it works...

Consider the following code line:

```
XamlServices.Save(xw, ab);
```

XamlServices provides services for the common XAML tasks of reading XAML and writing an object graph, or reading an object and writing out an XAML file. This statement reads an ActivityBuilder object and writes XAML to an XamlWriter object.

We use ActivityBuilder as an activity wrapper so that the output XAML is a loadable workflow. In other words, if we save, say, a Sequence activity to an XamlWriter directly, then the output XML workflow will be unloadable for further use.

Loading up a WF program from an XAML file

In this task, we will run a WF program by loading it from an XAML file.

How to do it...

1. **Create a workflow project**:

    Create a new **Workflow Console Application** under the Chapter01 solution and name the project as LoadUpWorkflowFromXML.

2. **Author a workflow**:

Author the `Workflow1.xaml` file; this workflow will print a string to console as shown in the following screenshot:

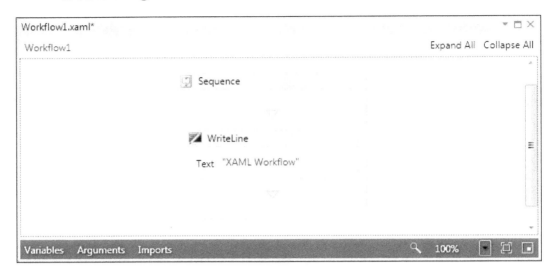

3. **Create code to load up the workflow instance from an XAML string**:

Open `Program.cs` file and change code as follow:

```
using System;
using System.Activities;
using System.Activities.Statements;
using System.IO;
using System.Collections;
using System.Text;
using System.Activities.XamlIntegration;

namespace LoadUpWorkflowFromXML {
    class Program {
        static void Main(string[] args) {
            string filePath=          @"C:\WF4Cookbook\Chapter01\
LoadUpWFFromXML\Workflow1.xaml";
            string tempString="";
            StringBuilder xamlWFString = new StringBuilder();
            StreamReader xamlStreamReader =
                new StreamReader(filePath);
            while (tempString != null){
                tempString = xamlStreamReader.ReadLine();
                if (tempString != null) {
                    xamlWFString.Append(tempString);
```

```
                    }
                }
                Activity wfInstance = ActivityXamlServices.Load(
                    new StringReader(xamlWFString.ToString()));
                WorkflowInvoker.Invoke(wfInstance);
            }
        }
    }
```

 We may need to change the file path
according to our real environment.

4. **Run it**:

   Set `LoadUpWorkflowFromXML` as **Startup** project. Press *Ctrl+F5* to build and run
   the workflow without debugging. The application should run in a console window and
   print the message as shown in the following screenshot:

How it works...

We use the following code block to read a workflow XML string from file and store the string in
`xamlWFString`:

```
string filePath=            @"C:\WF4Cookbook\Chapter01\LoadUpWFFromXML\
Workflow1.xaml";
string tempString="";
StringBuilder xamlWFString = new StringBuilder();
StreamReader xamlStreamReader =
new StreamReader(filePath);
while (tempString != null)
{
    tempString = xamlStreamReader.ReadLine();
    if (tempString != null)
    {
        xamlWFString.Append(tempString);
    }
}
```

Then, using the following statement, `ActivityXamlServices` reads the XML workflow and builds up a workflow object graph:

```
Activity wfInstance = ActivityXamlServices.Load(
                    new StringReader(xamlWFString.ToString()));
```

Testing a WF program with a unit test framework

In this task, we will create a Test Project to do unit testing for a WF program.

How to do it...

1. **Add a Test Project to the solution**:

   Add a **Test Project** to the `Chapter01` solution and name the project as `UnitTestForWFProgram` as shown in the following screenshot:

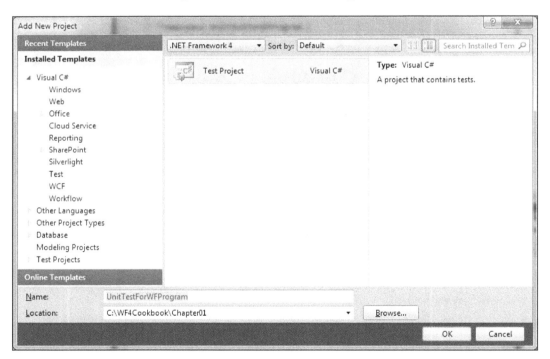

2. **Add a workflow file to the Test Project**:

Add a workflow activity to this project. Right-click the newly created Test Project, then go to **Add** | **New Items...** | **Workflow** | **Activity** and name the activity as `WorkflowForTest.xaml`. In the opening WF designer, create an `OutArgument` as **OutMessage**. Next, drag an **Assign** activity to the Designer panel and assign the string **"Test Message"** to the **OutMessage** argument as shown in the following screenshot:

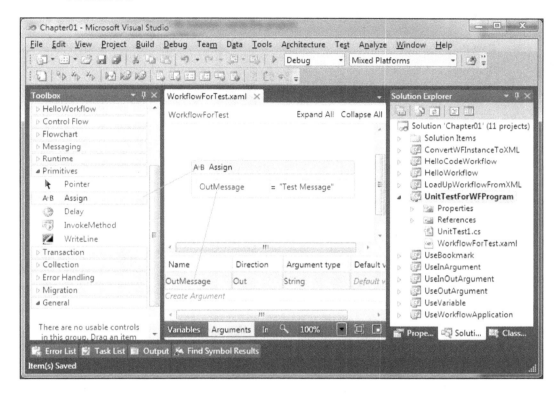

 In WF4, workflow is actually an Activity class. We could see "Workflow" as a conception from a macroeconomic viewpoint, while considering "Activity" as a development concept.

3. **Create unit test code**:

Open the `UnitTest1.cs` file and fill the file with following code:

```
using Microsoft.VisualStudio.TestTools.UnitTesting;
using System.Activities;

namespace UnitTestForWFProgram {
    [TestClass]
    public class UnitTest1 {
```

```
                    [TestMethod]
                    public void TestMethod1() {
                        var output =
                            WorkflowInvoker.Invoke(new WorkflowForTest());
                        Assert.AreEqual("Test Message",
                                        output["OutMessage"]);
                    }
                }
            }
```

4. **Run it:**

   Set `UnitTestForWorkflow` as **Startup** project. Press *Ctrl+F5* to build and run the test without debugging as shown in the following screenshot:

	Test run completed	Results: 1/1 passed;	Item(s) checked: 0	
	Result	Test Name	Project	Error Message
☐	Passed	TestMethod1	UnitTestForWFPro	

How it works...

In the preceding code snippet, `[TestClass]` indicates it is a unit test class, whereas `[TestMethod]` indicates a test method. When the Test Project runs, the test method will be executed automatically.

There's more...

In real application development, we can also create a separate Unit Test project and add a reference to the target project.

Debugging a WF program

In this task, we will debug a WF program.

How to do it...

1. **Create a workflow project**:

   Create a new **Workflow Console Application** project under the `Charpter01` solution. Name the project as `DebugWFProgram`. In the opening WF designer panel, author a workflow as shown in the following screenshot:

2. **Create workflow host code**:

Open `Program.cs` file and change the code to:

```
using System.Activities;
using System.Activities.Statements;

namespace DebugWFProgram{
    class Program{
        static void Main(string[] args){
            WorkflowInvoker.Invoke(new Workflow1()
            {
                InMessage="In Message"
            });
        }
    }
}
```

3. **Set a debug break point**:

   Right-click an activity and select **Breadpoint | Insert Breakpoint** to add debug break point.

4. **Debug it**:

   Press *F5* to debug the WF Program; we can refer the following screenshot:

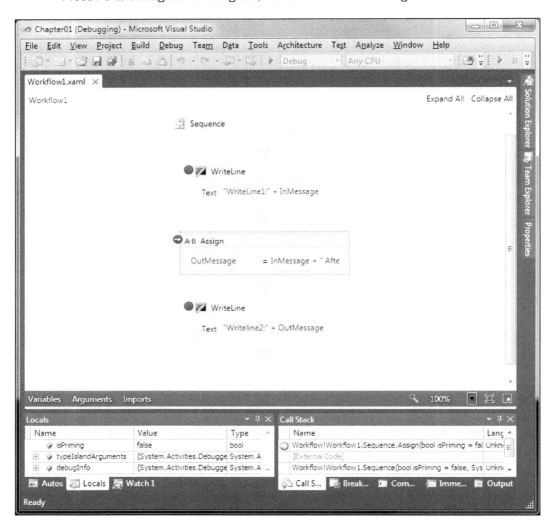

There's more...

We can also debug an XAML workflow. Open Workflow with the XML editor, insert some breakpoints, then press *F5*; we will see the breakpoints as shown in the following screenshot:

2
Built-in Flow Control Activities

In this chapter we will cover:

- ▶ Using the Foreach Activity
- ▶ A number guessing game in Sequence
- ▶ A number guessing game in a flowchart
- ▶ Using the `InvokeMethod` activity
- ▶ Using the `Switch<T>` activity in Sequence workflows
- ▶ Using the `FlowSwitch<T>` activity
- ▶ Using the Parallel activity
- ▶ Using `ParallelForEach<T>` activity
- ▶ Using the Pick activity
- ▶ Handling errors

Introduction

The Flow is the center of workflow itself, and how to control the Flow is what we will see in this chapter. WF is a lot like an imperative programming language such as C# when it comes to flow control; we have many similar concepts in WF4 such as "if-else", "foreach", "switch", "try-catch", and so on. Additionally, there are some other flow control activities that enable us to control workflow easily and efficiently such as the Parallel activity, Pick activity, ParallelForEach<T> activity, and so on.

In C#, we use language control key words to control everything. In WF4, this is slightly different. When we are developing a real workflow application, we will still write business logic in .NET code and build it out as DLL files so that we can reuse it everywhere. WF4 has two different types of workflow—Sequence workflow and Flowchart workflow. The famous State Machine workflow will be released in .NET Framework 4.5.

Using the Foreach activity

In this task, we will use the `Foreach` activity to traverse a person-type object.

How to do it...

1. **Create a Workflow Console Application project**:

   Create a new Workflow Console Application project and name it `UsingForeachActivity`. We can refer to the following screenshot:

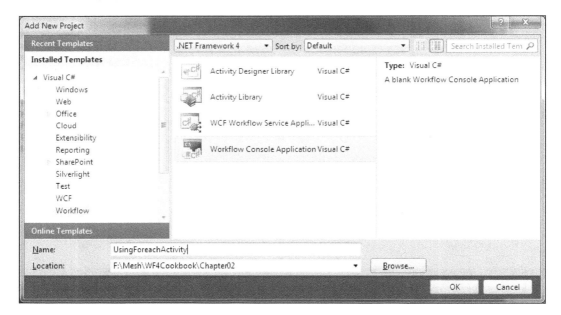

2. **Create a** `Person` **class file**:

   Add a new class file to the project, name the file `Person.cs`, fill the file with the following code, and save and build the project.

   ```
   namespace UsingForeachActivity {
       public class Person {
           public string Name { get; set; }
           public int Age { get; set; }
           public Person(string name, int age) {
               this.Name = name;
               this.Age = age;
           }
           public override string ToString() {
               return "Name:" + this.Name + " "
                   + " Age:" + this.Age;
           }
       }
   }
   ```

3. **Import** the `UsingForeachActivity` **namespace to the workflow**:

   In the bottom of workflow designer, click **Imports** and import the `UsingForeachActivity` namespace by using the drop-down list at the top of the Imports panel and pressing the *Enter* key.

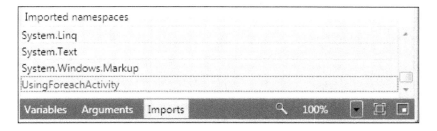

4. **Create a variable named** `people`:

   Open `Workflow1.xaml` in workflow designer, drag a Sequence activity to the designer panel, and then create a `List<Person>` type variable named `people` in the Sequence scope. To add a variable, we first need to click the variable button at the bottom of the screen then add the name in the name column. Next, in the **Variable type** drop-down, select **Browse for Types...**. Expand `mscorlib[4.0.0.0]` and select `System.Collections.Generic.List<T>`. Click **Browse for Types...** select **Person**. We can see the following screenshot:

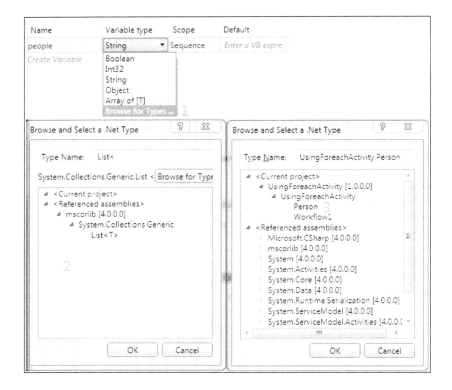

   Input the following VB Expression code in the **Default Expression** textbox of the variable `people`:

```
New List(Of Person) From
{
    New Person("Andrew", 26),
    New Person("Jophy", 25),
    New Person("Steven", 29)
}
```

5. **Author a workflow**:

Add a Sequence activity to the designer panel, and then add a `ForEach<T>` activity to the Sequence activity. Click `ForEach<T>`, in its **Properties** panel browse for the **TypeArgument** property, and select Person.

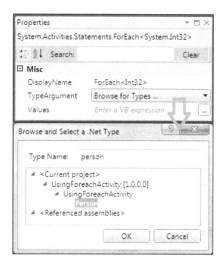

Input **From a In people** in the value expression. Next, drag a `WriteLine` to the body of `ForEach<Person>`. Set the expression textbox of `WriteLine` to `item.ToString` as shown in the following screenshot:

6. **Run it**:

Press *Ctrl+F5* to run the project without debugging and a console application will show the result:

How it works...

When the workflow project is created, the following code in the `Program.cs` file will be generated automatically:

```
static void Main(string[] args) {
    WorkflowInvoker.Invoke(new Workflow1());
}
```

Therefore, there is no need to add any code to the `Program.cs` file. The Foreach activity is similar to the foreach keyword in C#.

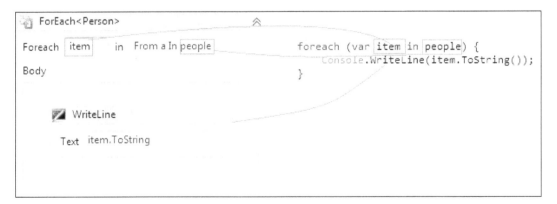

There's more...

Currently, we can use only VB expressions, but we may have C# expressions in the future.

A number guessing game in Sequence

In this task, we will create a guess number game in the Sequence activity. This task will also demonstrate the usage of the `DoWhile` and `IfElse` activities.

How to do it...

1. **Create a workflow project**:

   Create a Workflow Console Application and name it `GuessNumberGameInSequence`.

2. **Create a ReadNumberActivity to receive your guess number**:

   Create a new code file, name it `ReadNumberActivity.cs`, and fill the file with the following code:

```
using System;
using System.Activities;
namespace GuessNumberGameInSequence {
    public sealed class ReadNumberActivity : CodeActivity {
        public OutArgument<int> OutNumber { get; set; }
        protected override void Execute(CodeActivityContext
context) {
            OutNumber.Set(context, Int32.Parse(Console.
ReadLine()));
        }
    }
}
```

   Save and build the project so that we can use this activity in workflow designer.

3. **Author a workflow**:

Open `Workflow1.xaml` in workflow designer. Author the workflow as shown in the following screenshot:

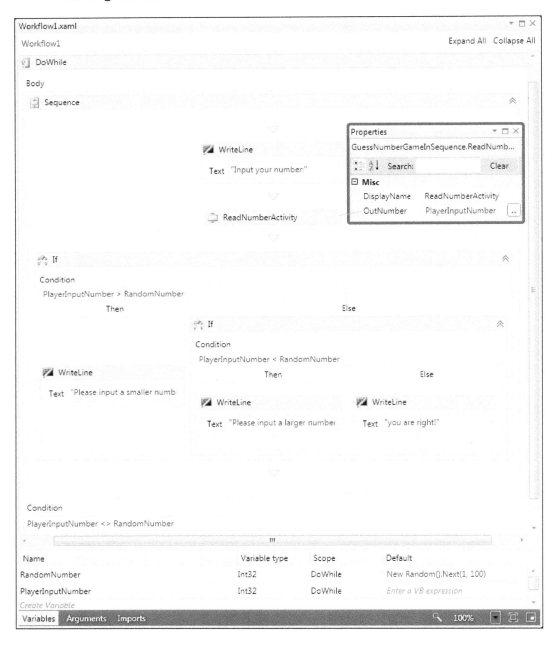

4. **Run it**:

   Set project `GuessNumberGameInSequence` as StartUp project. Press *CTRL+F5* to build and run the workflow without debugging. The application should run in a console window and print the following messages:

How it works...

When the workflow starts running, a random number will be generated and stored in the Variable named `RandomNumber`. First, the workflow will print **Input your number**: to the command console. In the `ReadNumberActivity`, the workflow will stop to wait our guess. After we input an integer number, workflow will compare our input number and the generated number, and will decide if we have made the right guess. If we do not input the right number, the workflow will give us a hint that we should input a larger or smaller number next time. As soon as we input the correct number, the workflow will then print **you are right!** to the command console.

Please note that in real workflow applications we should not use such a `ReadNumberActivity` because the `ReadNumberActivity` blocks the workflow execution. One best practice of creating an activity is writing code that will not block the workflow execution—for example, customizing an activity inherited from `NativeActivity` and creating a bookmark in the customized activity. We will create a bookmark activity in *Chapter 5, Custom Activities*.

A number guessing game using a flowchart

The flowchart was not invented in WF4. On the contrary, this type of diagram has a long history. The flowchart was first introduced by Frank Gilbreth in 1921 and he created a tool to use the flowchart in an industrial engineering curriculum.

As a programmer, you may already have experience in using a flowchart to draw an algorithm or process.

In this task, we will create a number guessing game using a flowchart. This task will also demonstrate the usage of the `FlowDecision` activity.

How to do it...

1. **Create a workflow project**:

   Create a Workflow Console Application and name it `GuessNumberGameInFlowChart`.

2. **Create a ReadNumberActivity to receive the guess number**:

   Create a new code file, name it `ReadNumberActivity.cs`, and fill the file with the following code:

   ```
   using System;
   using System.Activities;
   namespace GuessNumberGameInFlowChart {
       public sealed class ReadNumberActivity : CodeActivity {
           public OutArgument<int> OutNumber { get; set; }
           protected override void Execute(
               CodeActivityContext context) {
               OutNumber.Set(context,
                           Int32.Parse(Console.ReadLine()));
           }
       }
   }
   ```

   Save and build the project so that we can use this activity in workflow designer.

3. **Author a workflow**:

   Open `Workflow1.xaml` in workflow designer. Author the workflow as shown in the following screenshot:

Click the `ReadNumberActivity` activity and set its properties as:

4. **Run it**:

    Set `GuessNumberGameInFlowChart` as StartUp project. Press *CTRL+F5* to build and run the workflow without debugging.

How it works...

If you have finished both this and previous tasks, you may have already found out that we can create workflow by using Sequence workflow or Flowchart workflow. The question is what should we choose—Sequence or Flowchart. The rule is simple: if our workflow has many backward transitions, we should use Flowchart, otherwise, we should use Sequence workflow.

There's more

WF4.0 doesn't provide the famous State Machine workflow. In fact, we can create State Machine workflow by using Flowchart. However, there are many voices that demand a real State Machine workflow in WF4.0. So, Microsoft will provide the State Machine workflow in .NET Framework 4.5(WF4.5).

Using the InvokeMethod activity

In this task, we will use the `InvokeMethod` activity to invoke various kinds of methods.

How to do it...

1. **Create a workflow project**:

    Create a Workflow Console Application and name the project as `UsingInvokeMethodActivityInCode`.

2. **Create a class with various kinds of method:**

   Add a new class file to the project and name it `TestClass.cs`. Then fill the file with the following code:

```
using System;
public class TestClass {
    public void Method() {
        Console.WriteLine("Hello, message from Method()");
    }
    public void Method(string message1, string message2) {
        Console.WriteLine
            ("Hello, your message1 is:" + message1);
        Console.WriteLine
            ("Hello, this is your message2:" + message2);
    }
    public string MethodWithReturn(string message1,
                                   string message2) {
        return "message1:" + message1 +
            " " + "message2:" + message2;
    }
    public void MethodWithRef(string message1,
                              string message2,
                              ref string resultMessage) {
        resultMessage = "message1:" + message1 +
            " " + "message2:" + message2;
    }
    public void Method<T1, T2>(T1 param1, T2 param2) {
        Console.WriteLine
            ("The type of T1 is:" + typeof(T1));
        Console.WriteLine
            ("The value of param1 is:" + param1.ToString());
        Console.WriteLine
            ("The type of T2 is:" + typeof(T2));
        Console.WriteLine
            ("The value of param2 is:" + param2.ToString());
    }
    public static string StaticMethod(string message1,
                                      string message2) {
        return "message1:" + message1 +
            " " + "message2:" + message2;
    }
}
```

3. **Author a code workflow**:

Open `Program.cs` file and fill the file with the following code:

```
using System;
using System.Activities;
using System.Activities.Statements;
using System.Activities.Expressions;
namespace UsingInvokeMethodActivityInCode {
    class Program {
        static void Main(string[] args) {
            WorkflowInvoker.Invoke(CreateInvokeMethodWF());
        }
        static Activity CreateInvokeMethodWF() {
            TestClass testClass = new TestClass();
            Variable<string> resultValue = new Variable<string>();
            return new Sequence() {
                Variables = { resultValue },
                Activities ={
                    new WriteLine(){Text="...Invoke void
                    Method()"},
                    new InvokeMethod(){
                        TargetObject= new InArgument<TestClass>
                                        (aec=>testClass),
                        MethodName="Method",
                    },
                    new WriteLine(){
                        Text="...Invoke void Method(string"+
                            "message1,string message2)"},
                    new InvokeMethod(){
                        TargetObject= new InArgument<TestClass>
                                        (aec=>testClass),
                        MethodName="Method",
                        Parameters={
                            new InArgument<string>("This is
                                                    message1"),
                            new InArgument<string>("This is
                                                    message2")
                        }
                    },
                    new WriteLine(){
                        Text="...Invoke string MethodWithReturn"+
                        "(string message1, string message2)"},
                    new InvokeMethod<string>{
                        TargetObject=new InArgument<TestClass>
                                        (aec=>testClass),
```

```
        MethodName="MethodWithReturn",
        Parameters={
            new InArgument<string>("This is
                                    message1"),
            new InArgument<string>("This is
                                    message2")
        },
        Result=resultValue
    },
    new WriteLine(){
        Text=new InArgument<string>
            (ctx=>resultValue.Get(ctx))},
    new WriteLine()
        {Text="...Invoke void MethodWithRef"+
            "(string message1, string message2,"+
            "ref string resultMessage)"},
    new InvokeMethod(){
        TargetObject=new InArgument<TestClass>
                                (aec=>testClass),
        MethodName="MethodWithRef",
        Parameters={
            new InArgument<string>("This is
                                    message1"),
            new InArgument<string>("This is
                                    message2"),
            new InOutArgument<string>(resultValue)
        }
    },
    new WriteLine(){
        Text=new InArgument<string>
            (ctx=>resultValue.Get(ctx))},
    new WriteLine(){
        Text="...Invoke void Method<T1, T2>"+
        "(T1 param1, T2 param2)"},
    new InvokeMethod(){
        TargetObject=new InArgument<TestClass>
                                (aec=>testClass),
        MethodName="Method",
        GenericTypeArguments={
            typeof(string),
            typeof(int)
        },
        Parameters={
            new InArgument<string>("string
                                    message"),
```

```
                                    new InArgument<int>(123)
                            }
                    },
                    new WriteLine(){
                            Text="...Invoke static string"+
                            "StaticMethod(string message1, string
                                            message2)"},
                    new InvokeMethod<string>{
                            TargetType=typeof(TestClass),
                            MethodName="StaticMethod",
                            Parameters={
                                    new InArgument<string>("This is
                                                    message1"),
                                    new InArgument<string>("This is
                                                    message2")
                            },
                            Result=resultValue
                    },
                    new WriteLine(){
                            Text=new InArgument<string>
                                    (ctx=>resultValue.Get(ctx))}
            }
        };
    }
  }
}
```

4. **Run It**:

    Set `UsingInvokeMethodActivityInCode` as StartUp project. Press *CTRL+F5* to build and run the workflow without debugging. We will see the following:

```
C:\Windows\system32\cmd.exe

...Invoke void Method()
Hello, message from Method()
...Invoke void Method(stringmessage1,string message2)
Hello, your message1 is:This is message1
Hello, this is your message2:This is message2
...Invoke string MethodWithReturn(string message1, string message2)
message1:This is message1 message2:This is message2
...Invoke void MethodWithRef(string message1, string message2,ref string resultMessage)
message1:This is message1 message2:This is message2
...Invoke void Method<T1, T2>(T1 param1, T2 param2)
The type of T1 is:System.String
The value of param1 is:string message
The type of T2 is:System.Int32
The value of param2 is:123
...Invoke static stringStaticMethod(string message1, string message2)
message1:This is message1 message2:This is message2
Press any key to continue . . .
```

How it works...

As we can see, there is a lot of code in this task, but we don't have to understand all of the code at one time. We can read and understand it piece by piece. For instance, in `TestClass`, we have the following method:

```
public void Method() {
    Console.WriteLine("Hello, message from Method()");
}
```

In the workflow, we want to call the following method:

```
new InvokeMethod(){
    TargetObject= new InArgument<TestClass>(aec=>testClass),
    MethodName="Method",
}
```

Here is the explanation of the important properties of `InvokeMethod` activity:

- ▶ `MethodName`: Assign the method name to this property
- ▶ `TargetObject`: When we want to invoke non-static methods, we need first to create an object that contains the method to execute
- ▶ `TargetType`: When we want to invoke static methods, we specify the type that contains the static method to execute
- ▶ `GenericTypeArguments`: When we want to invoke a generic method, we specify generic types in this collection

  Here is a sample from step 3:

  ```
  newInvokeMethod(){
  TargetObject=new InArgument<TestClass>(aec=>testClass),
  MethodName="Method",
  GenericTypeArguments={
  typeof(string),
  typeof(int)
  },
  Parameters={
  newInArgument<string>("string message"),
  newInArgument<int>(123)
  }
  },
  ```

- ▶ `Parameters`: The parameter collection of the method to be invoked
- ▶ `Result`: The return value of the method execution

There's more

We can use the `InvokeMethod` activity in the visual workflow:

▶ **Invoke 'void Method()'** (C# method):

A method without parameters and return type:

```
public void Method() {
    Console.WriteLine("'void Method()' is called");
}
```

`InvokeMethod` activity:

```
Invoke 'void Method()'

TargetType    (null)              ▼

TargetObject  New TestClass()

MethodName    Method
```

▶ **Invoke 'void Method(var1,var2)'** (C# method):

A method with two parameters:

```
public void Method(string message1, string message2) {
    Console.WriteLine("'void Method(string message1, string
message2)' is called");
    Console.WriteLine
        ("Hello, this is your message1:" + message1);
    Console.WriteLine
        ("Hello, this is your message2:" + message2);
}
```

`InvokeMethod` activity:

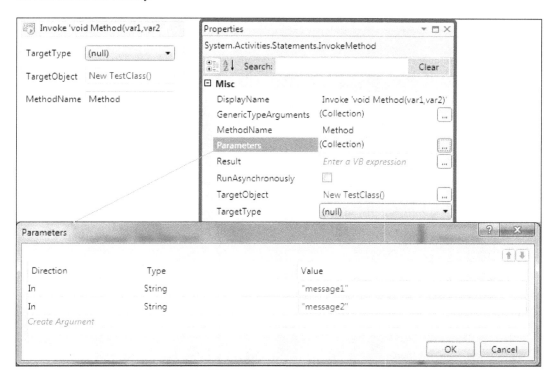

> **Invoke 'string MethodWithReturn(var1,var2)'** (C# method):

A method with two parameters and String return type:

```
public string MethodWithReturn(string message1,
                                string message2) {
    Console.WriteLine("'string MethodWithReturn(string
message1,string message2)' is called");
    return "message1:" + message1 +
        " " + "message2:" + message2;
}
```

`InvokeMethod` activity:

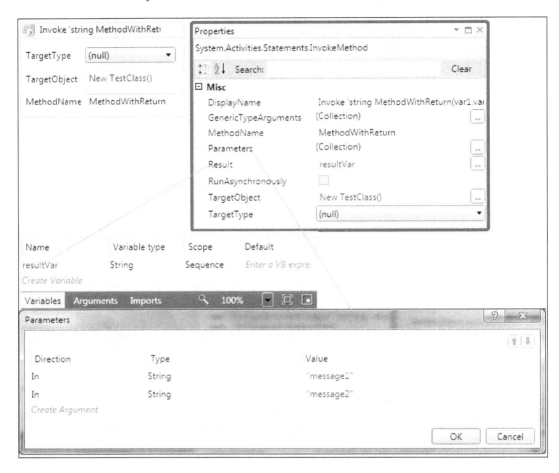

> ▸ **Invoke 'void MethodWithRef'** (C# method):

```
public void MethodWithRef(string message1,
                          string message2,
                          ref string resultMessage) {
    resultMessage = "message1:" + message1 +
        " " + "message2:" + message2;
}
```

`InvokeMethod` activity:

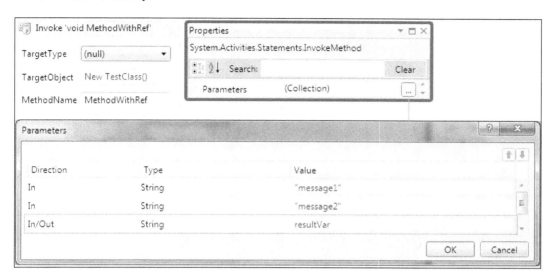

Please note that the `resultVar` must be **In/Out** direction parameter to work with the `ref` parameter.

▸ **Invoke generic method** (C# method):

```
public void Method<T1, T2>(T1 param1, T2 param2) {
    Console.WriteLine
        ("The type of T1 is:" + typeof(T1));
    Console.WriteLine
        ("The value of param1 is:" + param1.ToString());
    Console.WriteLine
        ("The type of T2 is:" + typeof(T2));
    Console.WriteLine
        ("The value of param2 is:" + param2.ToString());
}
```

`InvokeMethod` activity:

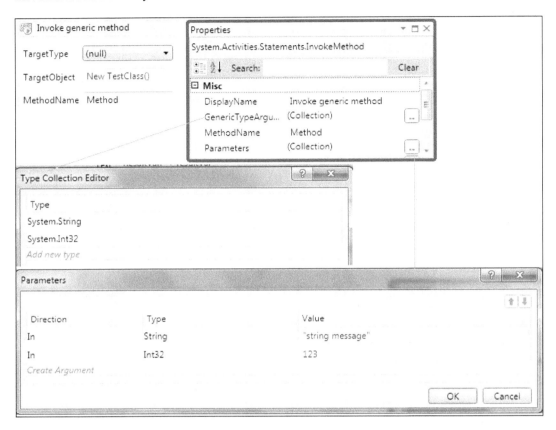

- **Invoke static method** (C# method):

```
public static string StaticMethod(string message1,
                                  string message2) {
    return "message1:" + message1 +
        " " + "message2:" + message2;
}
```

`InvokeMethod` activity:

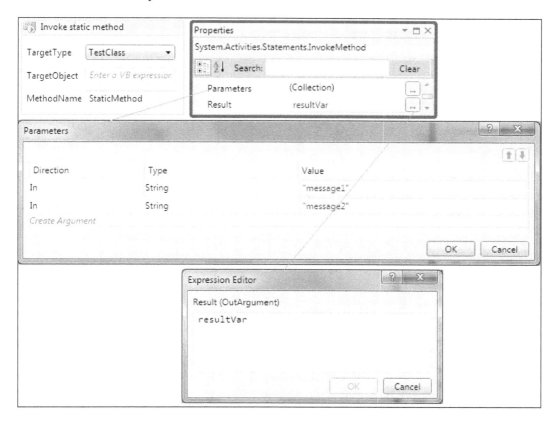

Using the Switch<T> activity in Sequence workflow

In this task, we will inspect the usage of the Switch activity in Sequence workflow. The `Switch<T>` activity will not only accept a *string* as a condition but also an *object*.

How to do it...

1. **Create a Workflow project**:

   Create a new Workflow Console Application project and name the project as `UsingSwitchActivityInSequenceWorkflow`.

2. **Create a test class file** `Product.cs`:

Add a new class to the project, name it `Product.cs`, and fill the file with the following code:

```
using System;
using System.ComponentModel;
namespace UsingSwitchActivityInSequenceWorkflow {
    [TypeConverter(typeof(ProductConverter))]
    public class Product {
        public string ProductName { get; set; }
        public Guid ProductId { get; set; }
        public Product() {
            this.ProductName = "Defualt Name";
            this.ProductId =Guid.NewGuid();
        }
        public Product(string productName, Guid productId) {
            this.ProductName = productName;
            this.ProductId = productId;
        }
        public override bool Equals(object obj) {
            Product product = obj as Product;
            if (product != null) {
                return string.Equals(this.ProductId,
                                        product.ProductId);
            }
            return false;
        }
        public override int GetHashCode() {
            if (this.ProductName != null) {
                return this.ProductName.GetHashCode();
            }
            return 0;
        }
    }
}
```

3. **Add a class converter to the project**:

Add another new class to the project, name it `ProductConverter.cs`, and fill the file with following code:

```
using System;
using System.ComponentModel;
using System.Globalization;
namespace UsingSwitchActivityInSequenceWorkflow {
    public class ProductConverter : TypeConverter {
```

```csharp
public override bool CanConvertFrom(
    ITypeDescriptorContext context,
    System.Type sourceType) {
    return sourceType == typeof(string);
}
public override object ConvertFrom(
    ITypeDescriptorContext context,
    CultureInfo culture,
    object value) {
    if (value == null) {
        return null;
    }
    if (value is string) {
        return new Product() {
            ProductName = (string)value,
            ProductId = Guid.NewGuid();

        };
    }
    return base.ConvertFrom(context, culture, value);
}
public override object ConvertTo(
    ITypeDescriptorContext context,
    CultureInfo culture,
    object value,
    System.Type destinationType) {
    if (destinationType == typeof(string)) {
        if (value != null) {
            return ((Product)value).ProductName;
        } else {
            return null;
        }
    }
    return base.ConvertTo(
        context,
        culture,
        value,
        destinationType);
    }
    }
}
```

The WF4 Switch<T> activity will use this class to convert the `Product` class from/to string. Before moving to step 4, we need to build the project so that the workflow can find the `Product` and `ProductConverter` type.

4. **Author a workflow**:

   Open the `Workflow1.xaml` file created by default. Import the `UsingSwitchActivityInSequenceWorkflow` namespace. Drag a **Sequence** activity to the designer panel and next drag a **Switch<T>** into the sequence. A dialog will show up asking for type; choose *Product* type for it. See the following screenshot:

5. **Run it**:

Set `UsingSwitchActivityInSequenceWorkflow` as StartUp project. Press *CTRL+F5* to build and run the workflow without debugging. A console application will show the result:

How it works...

Traditionally, in C#, a switch statement can operate only on primitive types such as `Boolean`, `Int32`, `String`, and `enumeration` types. In WF4, a Switch activity can operate on a user-defined type at runtime.

To enable this interesting feature, we must perform the following steps:

1. Create a type converter class to convert an object of user-defined type to a string and a string to object.

2. Override the following two methods of user-defined classes: `public override bool Equals(object obj)` and `public override int GetHashCode()`.

We can then see the `Product` class for the implementation sample.

There's more

We can change expression to let the sample project print another result—for example, `New Product("BMP Software", Guid.NewGuid())`.

Using the FlowSwitch<T> activity

In the flowchart, we should use the `FlowSwitch` Activity instead of the `Switch<T>` activity, which we used in the previous task. In this task, we will create a flowchart workflow using the `FlowSwitch<T>` activity. This switch activity will operate on a string.

How to do it...

1. **Create a workflow project**:

Create a new Workflow Console Application project and name the project as `UsingFlowSwitchActivity`.

2. **Author a workflow**:

Open `Workflow1.xaml` and author a workflow as shown in the following screenshot. Please note that when we drag the `Flowswitch` activity to the flowchart, we will be shown a dialog to choose the type. In this task, we have chosen `String`.

When we add the case links, please do not to add quotation marks ("") around the case branch. Because the `Flowswitch` activity will not only operate on strings but also other types.

3. **Run it**:

Set `UsingFlowChartActivity` as StartUp project. Press *CTRL+F5* to build and run the workflow without debugging. A console application will show the result.

How it works

Like the switch key word in C#, the `FlowSwitch<T>` activity is a Flowchart condition node that handles multiple selections by passing control to one of the branch activities. Please note that if the flow branching requires only two paths, we should use the `FlowDescision` activity instead.

See Also

A number guessing game in a flowchart.

Using the Parallel activity

In this task, we will create a sample that will use the Parallel activity. The Parallel activity can execute its child activities in parallel, asynchronously.

How to do it...

1. **Create a workflow project**:

Create a new Workflow Console Application under solution `Chapter02` and name the project as `UsingParallelActivity`.

2. **Create a workflow**:

   Open `Workflow1.xaml` and create a workflow as shown in the following screenshot:

Set the properties of both Delay activities:

3. **Run it**:

Set `UsingParallelActivity` as StartUp project. Press *CTRL+F5* to build and run the workflow without debugging.

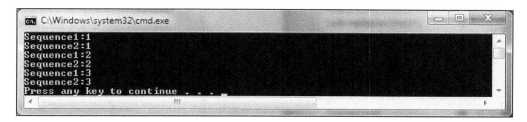

```
C:\Windows\system32\cmd.exe
Sequence1:1
Sequence2:1
Sequence1:2
Sequence2:2
Sequence1:3
Sequence2:3
Press any key to continue . . .
```

How it works...

Workflow execution starts from **Sequence1**, then there is a delay of 5 seconds and the execution of Parallel will shift to the **Sequence2** branch immediately. Now **Sequence2** will delay for 5 seconds and the execution shift to the **Sequence1** branch again, and now, both **Sequence1** and **Sequence2** are in a delaying state. The whole Parallel activity will wait there until one of them awakes.

> The embedded parallel branches are scheduled and run asynchronously, but they do not run on separate threads. So, each successive branch will execute only when the previous branch completes or goes idle.

Using the ParallelForEach<T> activity

`ParallelForEach<T>` is actually a special `ForEach<T>` activity. The difference between `ParallelForEach<T>` and `ForEach<T>` is that `ParallelForEach<T>`'s embedded statements are scheduled and run asynchronously. `ParallelForEach<T>` itself is akin to a Parallel activity for its child activities. Let's create a sample to see how it works.

How to do it...

1. **Create a workflow project**:

Create a new Workflow Console Application under solution `Chapter02` and name the project `UsingParallelForEachActivity`.

2. **Create a workflow**:

Open `Workflow1.xaml` and author a workflow as shown in the following screenshot:

Set the properties of both Delay activities:

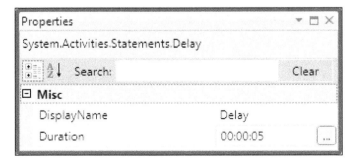

3. **Run it**:

Set `UsingParallelForEachActivity` as StartUp project. Press *CTRL+F5* to build and run the workflow without debugging. We can refer the following screenshot:

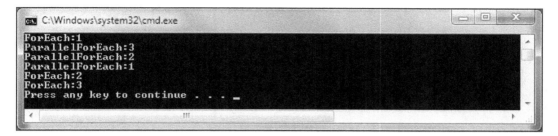

How it works...

We should find that the Delay activity in Seqence2 branch seems not to take effect at all. In fact, whenever the `ParallelForEach<Int32>`'s embedded statement goes idle, the next statement will be executed immediately rather than waiting there, that is why we call it the `ParallelForEach` activity.

Using the Pick activity

The Pick activity in WF4 is similar to the Listen activity in WF3. This activity will execute one of its parallel subactivities, and only one of its activities will be executed before the Pick activity completes. Typically, we use Pick to set up a time-out for an activity.

How to do it...

1. **Create a workflow project**:

Create a new Workflow Console Application and name it `UsingPickActivity`.

2. **Create a workflow**:

Create a workflow as shown in the following screenshot:

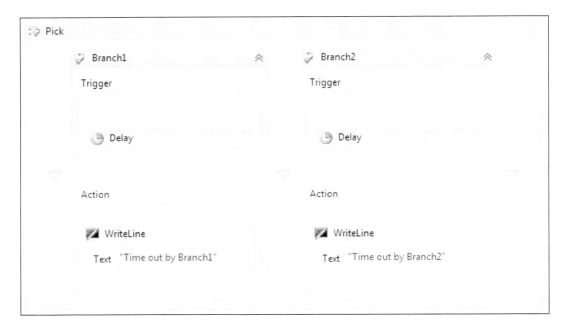

 We are not allowed to define variables in the Pick activity scope.

Set the Properties of the Delay activity of Branch1:

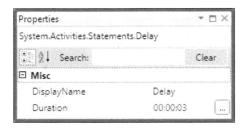

Set the Properties of the Delay activity of Branch2:

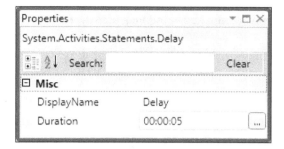

3. **Create a workflow host**:

   Open the `Program.cs` file and fill the file with following code:

```
using System;
using System.Activities;
using System.Activities.Statements;
using System.Threading;
namespace UsingPickActivity {
    class Program {
        static void Main(string[] args) {
            AutoResetEvent waitHandler =
                new AutoResetEvent(false);
            WorkflowApplication wfApp =
                new WorkflowApplication(new Workflow1());
            wfApp.Completed = (e) => waitHandler.Set();
            wfApp.Run();
            waitHandler.WaitOne();
        }
    }
}
```

4. **Run it**:

   Set `UsingPickActivity` as StartUp project, and press *Ctrl+F5* to run the workflow without debugging.

How it works...

In this workflow, there are two branches in the Pick activity. Each branch has a Delay activity—Branch1 is delayed by 3 seconds, whereas Branch2 is delayed by 5 seconds. At execution time, both branches are executed in parallel. When Branch1 completes, Branch2 is cancelled.

There's more

If we are already familiar with customized activities and bookmark, we can replace one of the Delay activity with a bookmark activity.

To create a bookmark:

1. Add a new code file to the project and name the file as `MyBookmark.cs`. Fill the file with the following code:

```
using System.Activities;
namespace UsingPickActivity {
    public class MyBookmark : NativeActivity<string> {
        [RequiredArgument]
        public InArgument<string> BookmarkName { get; set; }
        protected override void Execute(
            NativeActivityContext context) {
            context.CreateBookmark(BookmarkName.Get(context),
                new BookmarkCallback(OnResumeBookmark));
        }
        protected override bool CanInduceIdle {
            get { return true; }
        }
        public void OnResumeBookmark(
            NativeActivityContext context,
            Bookmark bookmark, object obj) {
            Result.Set(context, (string)obj);
        }
    }
}
```

   Save and build the project for us to be able to use this bookmark in workflow designer.

2. Open `Workflow1.xaml`. Click the left Trigger (Branch1) and create an `inputString` Variable. Create an `InArgument` named `BookmarkName`. We now need to replace the left Delay activity with our bookmark activity: `MyBookmark`. See the following screenshot:

Properties of `MyBookmark` activity:

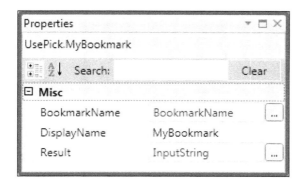

3. Change the host code in the `program.cs` file as follows:

```
///Pick Activity with bookmark Activity
string BMName = "StringInputBookmark";
AutoResetEvent waitHandler =
    new AutoResetEvent(false);
WorkflowApplication wfApp =
    new WorkflowApplication(new Workflow1() {
        BookmarkName = BMName
    });
wfApp.Completed = (e) => waitHandler.Set();
wfApp.Run();
wfApp.ResumeBookmark(BMName, Console.ReadLine());
waitHandler.WaitOne();
```

4. Set `UsingPickActivity` as StartUp project, and press *Ctrl+F5* to run the workflow without debugging. In the opening console application, we can either input a string or wait for 5 seconds, and the workflow will time out and terminate.

Handling errors

In this task, we are going to create a Sequence workflow with a `TryCatch` activity. There will be a dividend assigned with zero, and hence we can generate a divide-by-zero exception deliberately so that we can handle this error in a `TryCatch` activity.

How to do it...

1. **Create a workflow project**:

   Create a new Workflow Console Application and name it `ErrorHandling`.

2. **Create a code workflow**:

   Create a new class file and name it `ErrorHandlingWorkflow.cs`. Fill the file with the following code:

```
using System;
using System.Activities;
using System.Activities.Statements;
namespace ErrorHandling {
    public class ErrorHandlingWorkflow{
        public Activity GetInstance() {
            Variable<int> divisor = new Variable<int>("divisor",
                                                      10);
            Variable<int> dividend = new Variable<int>("dividend",
                                                       0);
            Variable<int> result = new Variable<int>("result");
```

```
            DelegateInArgument<DivideByZeroException> eia = new De
legateInArgument<DivideByZeroException>();
            Activity workflow = new Sequence() {
                Variables = { divisor, dividend, result },
                Activities ={
                    new TryCatch{
                        Try=new Assign{
                            To=new OutArgument<int>(result),
                            Value=new InArgument<int>(
                                aec=>divisor.Get(aec)/dividend.
                                                        Get(aec)
                            )
                        },
                        Catches={
                            new Catch<DivideByZeroException>{
                                Action=new ActivityAction<DivideBy
ZeroException>{
                                    Argument=eia,
                                    Handler=new Sequence{
                                        Activities={
                                            new
WriteLine{Text="Divide By Zero Exception"},
                                        }
                                    }
                                },
                            }
                        },
                        Finally=new WriteLine{Text="finally,calcul
ation done"}
                    }
                }
            };
            return workflow;
        }
    }
}
```

3. **Create host code**:

   Open `Program.cs` file and alter the code to:

   ```
   using System.Activities;
   namespace ErrorHandling {
       class Program {
           static void Main(string[] args) {
               ErrorHandlingWorkflow errorHandlingWorkflow=
                   new ErrorHandlingWorkflow();
               WorkflowInvoker.Invoke(errorHandlingWorkflow.
   GetInstance());
           }
       }
   }
   ```

4. **Run it**:

   Press *Ctrl+F5* to run the sample. We will be able to see a console application like this:

How it works...

The `TryCatch` activity in WF4 is pretty much like the "try catch" keywords in C#. They both have "try", "catch", and "finally", and they even share similar structure. With the `TryCatch` activity, we can use these keywords as follows:

```
new TryCatch{
       Try=//WF4 Activity
       Catch={}// Catch collection
       Finally= //WF4 Activity
}
```

Note that the `Finally` activity will not be executed unless the `Try` block or one of the `Catch` blocks completes.

3
Messaging and Transaction

This chapter will cover:

- ▶ Creating a pure WCF service
- ▶ Receiving and replying a WCF message
- ▶ Receiving and replying to a WCF message in code workflow
- ▶ Sending and receiving a reply to a WCF message
- ▶ Sending and receiving a reply to a WCF message in code workflow
- ▶ Using CancellationScope activity
- ▶ Performing a transaction by using TransactionScope activity
- ▶ Performing compensation by using Compensable activity
- ▶ Performing manual compensation by using Compensate activity
- ▶ Performing confirmation by using Confirm activity

Introduction

In a traditional imperative program language such as C#, if one wished to send/receive message to/from a remote location, one was expected to write a lot of code, have thorough knowledge of TCP/IP, HTTP, .Net Remoting, Web Service, and so on. Starting from .NET Framework 3.0, Microsoft launched WCF (Windows Communication Foundation). By using WCF, messaging has become an easy and flexible task. WF4 takes advantage of WCF and provides some out of the box messaging activities. In this chapter, we will focus on the built-in messaging activities shipped by WF4.

In the case of service host, though we can use the Local Web Development Server shipped with .NET Framework4.0 as the WCF host, I personally recommend the real IIS7.0 or IIS 7.5. For detailed IIS installation steps, we can refer to the documents from `http://learn.iis.net/page.aspx/85/installing-iis-7/`.

To make sure our application has permission to open a WCF HTTP port, we should run Visual Studio 2010 as administrator.

Creating a pure WCF service

In case one is new to WCF, he/she can use this task to become familiar with fundamental WCF concepts. In this task, we will create a simple WCF stock price service host in IIS 7.

How to do it...

1. **Create a IIS Application**:

   Right-click an IIS Site; we will see the menu shown in the following screenshot:

   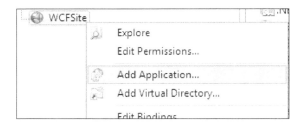

   Then create a `StockPriceService` application.

   Please remember its folder path. We will create files in this folder in the following steps.

   Please also note that the WCFSite should run in .NET Framework 4.0 application pool.

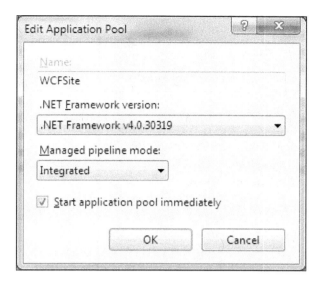

2. **Create WCF code**:

Create a new folder named App_Code in the application folder. Next, create a StockService.cs file in the App_Code folder. Fill the StockService.cs file with the following code:

```
using System;
using System.ServiceModel;
namespace StockPriceService {
    [ServiceContract]
    public interface IStockService {
        [OperationContract]
        double GetPrice(string ticket);
    }
    public class StockService : IStockService {
        public double GetPrice(string ticket) {
            return 94.85;
        }
    }
}
```

3. **Create an svc file**:

In the application folder, create a new file named StockService.svc and fill the file with the following code:

```
<%@ServiceHost   language=c#
                 Debug="true"
                 Service="StockPriceService.StockService"%>
```

4. **Create a config file**:

In the application folder, create the configuration file by the name of `Web.config`, and fill the configuration file with the following code:

```xml
<?xml version="1.0" encoding="utf-8" ?>
<configuration>
  <system.serviceModel>
    <services>
      <service name="StockPriceService.StockService"
               behaviorConfiguration="MEXServiceTypeBehavior">
        <endpoint address=""
                  binding="wsHttpBinding"
                  contract="StockPriceService.IStockService"/>
        <endpoint address="mex"
                  binding="mexHttpBinding"
                  contract="IMetadataExchange"/>
      </service>
    </services>
    <behaviors>
      <serviceBehaviors>
        <behavior name="MEXServiceTypeBehavior">
          <serviceMetadata httpGetEnabled="true" />
        </behavior>
      </serviceBehaviors>
    </behaviors>
  </system.serviceModel>
</configuration>
```

Please note that we must set the service and contract name correctly; refer to the code part that is highlighted in the preceding code snippet.

5. **Test it**:

If we have finished the above steps, in the IIS content panel we shall see the following:

Name	Type
App_Code	File Folder
StockService.svc	ASP.NET Web Service
Web.config	CONFIG File

We can test it in two ways.

    i.   *Using an internet browser*: Right-click the `StockService.svc` and click **Browse**.

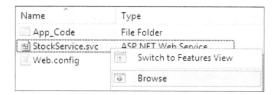

IIS will open the service in IE by default.

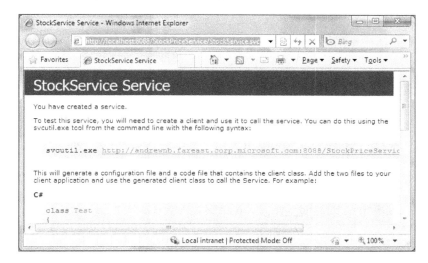

    ii.   *Using WCF Test Client*: By default, navigate to `C:\Program Files (x86)\Microsoft Visual Studio 10.0\Common7\IDE`. We should find the WCF Test Client, `WcfTestClient.exe`. If we have our Visual Studio 2010 installed in another path, we can type `wcftestclient` in the **Run** command box to search for the tool.

After we have found the tool, we will open it. Add the `StockPriceService` to the tool, double-click the `GetPrice()` method, and then click the **Invoke** button to get the result.

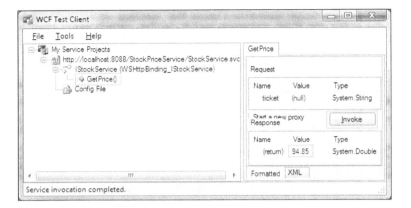

How it works...

To understand WCF, we need to understand the famous ABCs of WCF.

> ► **A** stands for **Address**. Because of A, the service client knows where to find the service; in this task the address is defined by the IIS site `http://localhost:8088/StockPriceService/StockService.svc`.

> ► **B** stands for **binding**. Because of B, the service client knows how to use the service. There are many binding types such as `basicHttpBinding`, `wsHttpBinding`, and so on. Different services use different binding types. In this task, we use `wsHttpBinding`. This is defined in the `web.config` file.

> ► **C** stands for **contract**. Because of C, the service client knows what content the service provides. In this task, we use the `IStockService` interface that is decorated with the `ServiceContract` attribute to define the WCF contract.

When the request comes, IIS will capture the request. IIS finds that the request is postfixed with `svc`. The following are the `httphandler` mappings:

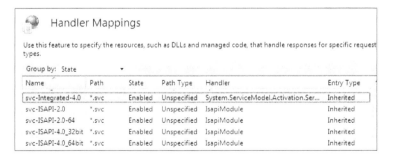

According to the `httphandler` mappings, IIS will use the appropriate handler to handle the WCF request. If it is the first running time of the WCF service, like an ASP.NET application, IIS will compile the .NET code and configure the file to DLLs. That is why the first request will take a little bit longer to get the response.

There's more

WCF (Windows Communication Foundation) is Microsoft's next-generation unified network programming model for building service-oriented applications. WCF enables us to build secure, reliable, and distributed solutions with ease. As this is a WF4 book, I am not going to elaborate on WCF. We can work through the following tasks based on the understanding from this task. Of course we will understand the following tasks better if we are already equipped with enough WCF knowledge.

Receiving and replying to a WCF message

In this task, we will create a workflow with **Receive** and **SendReply** activities, and run a workflow as a WCF service. This workflow will accept two integer numbers and return their sum to the caller. We will use WCF Test Client to test the service.

How to do it...

1. **Create a workflow project**:

   Create a new WCF Workflow Service Application project and name it `ReceiveAndReply`; refer to the following screenshot:

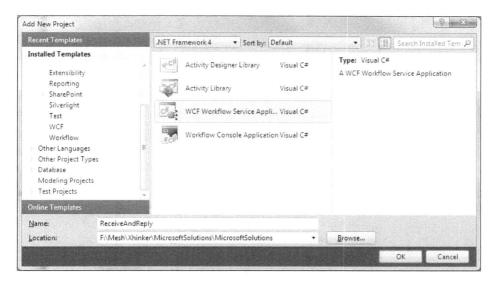

2. **Create a workflow**:

Open the default created `Service1.xamlx`. We need to perform the following actions:

i. Add two `Int32` type WF4 Variables x and y to the **Sequential Service** scope.

Name	Variable type	Scope	Default
y	Int32	Sequential Service	*Enter a VB expression*
x	Int32	Sequential Service	*Enter a VB expression*

ii. Click the **View parameter...** link of the `ReceiveRequest` activity and add two `Int32` type service parameters `xIn` and `yIn` as shown in the following screenshot:

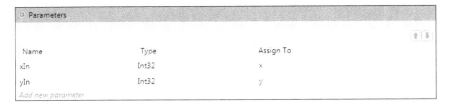

Name	Type	Assign To
xIn	Int32	x
yIn	Int32	y

iii. Right-click the `ReceiveRequest` activity and select **Properties**; the properties should be set as shown in the screenshot:

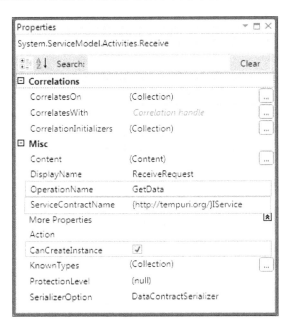

iv. Click the **View parameter...** link of the `SendResponse` activity and add an `Int32` type service parameter named `addResult`; refer to the following screenshot:

Now, we can save and close the workflow. The final workflow should be like this:

3. **Test it in WCFTestClient**:

We need to perform the following actions to test the WF service:

i. Right-click `Service1.xamlx` and select the **View** option in the browser; we should see the following:

  ii. Copy the following address (the port will be different in your computer): `http://localhost:11641/Service1.xamlx`. Add the service to `WCFTestClient`.

New to WCF Test Client?

By default, navigate to `C:\Program Files (x86)\Microsoft Visual Studio 10.0\Common7\IDE`. You will find the WCF Test Client, `WcfTestClient.exe`. If you have your Visual Studio 2010 installed in your own folder, you can type `wcftestclient` in the **Run** command box to search the tool.

  iii. Double-click the `GetData()` method, input two numbers for `xIn` and `yIn` respectively, and then click the **Invoke** button. If we can get the addition result, we have successfully created the workflow service.

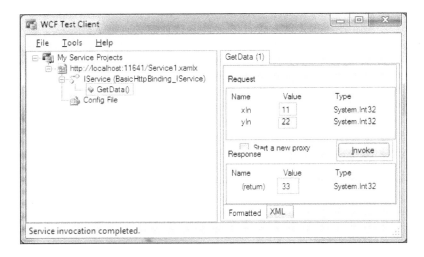

4. **Deploy the Workflow service in IIS**:

We need to perform the following actions to deploy the Workflow service in IIS:

  i. Add an IIS application under an IIS Site.

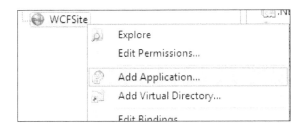

ii.   Set the application's **Physical path** to the project folder path:

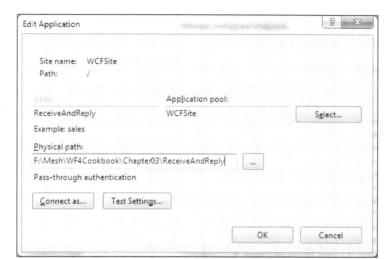

How it works...

When we create a WCF Workflow Service Application, Visual Studio 2010 will automatically create many things. There are two items we need to pay close attention to.

▶   The configuration file `Web.config`: When we deploy the workflow service to IIS, it will look for configuration information against the `Web.config` file automatically, just like the `Web.config` file in ASP.NET applications. We can also add or remove features by editing the `Web.config` file.

▶   `Service.xamlx`: We can notice that the postfix is `xamlx` instead of `xaml`. So, we may think, What is the difference between XAMLX workflow and XAMLX workflow? Well, XAMLX workflow is designed for IIS particularly. If we want to host workflow service in IIS, we need to create XAMLX workflow. But what we should do if we have already created many XAML workflows and still want to host it in IIS? The solution is simple: remove all `InArguments` and replace the XAML with XAMLX.

By performing these two steps, we can host an XAML workflow service in IIS too.

When the WCF request comes, IIS will capture the request and use xamlx-ISAPI to handle the request.

In the code behind, IIS uses `WorkflowServiceHost` as the workflow service host.

If we want to know how to create and host the workflow service with imperative code, we may refer to the next task.

Receiving and replying to a WCF message in code workflow

In this task, we will create a code workflow with **Receive** and **SendReply** activities, and will run the workflow as a WCF service. This workflow will accept two integer numbers and return the addition sum to the caller. This workflow is hosted in a console application rather than IIS. We will use WCF Test Client to test the service.

How to do it...

1. **Create a workflow Console Application project**:

   Create a new Workflow Console Application named `ReceiveAndReplyInCode`.

2. **Create the workflow in code**:

   Add a new class file to the project and name it `ReceiveAndReplyWorkflow.cs`. Fill the file with the following code:

```
using System;
using System.ServiceModel.Activities;
using System.Activities;
using System.ServiceModel;
using System.Activities.Statements;
namespace ReceiveAndReply {
    class ReceiveAndReplyWorkflow {
        public WorkflowService GetInstance() {
```

```
WorkflowService service;
Variable<int> x = new Variable<int> { Name = "x" };
Variable<int> y = new Variable<int> { Name = "y" };
Variable<int> addResult =
    new Variable<int> { Name = "addResult" };
Receive receive = new Receive {
    ServiceContractName = "ICalculateService",
    OperationName = "GetData",
    CanCreateInstance = true,
    Content = new ReceiveParametersContent {
        Parameters ={
            {"xIn",new OutArgument<int>(x) },
            {"yIn",new OutArgument<int>(y) }
        }
    }
};
Sequence workflow = new Sequence() {
    Variables = { x, y, addResult },
    Activities = {
        new WriteLine{Text="WF service is
                        starting..."},
        receive,
        new WriteLine{Text="receive request with two
                        numbers"},
        new WriteLine{
            Text=new InArgument<string>(aec=>
                "x="+x.Get(aec).ToString()+" y="+y.
                                        Get(aec)
            )
        },
        new Assign<int>{
            Value=new InArgument<int>(aec=>x.
                                Get(aec)+y.Get(aec)),
            To=new OutArgument<int>(addResult)
        },
        new WriteLine{
            Text=new InArgument<string>(aec=>
                "addResult="+addResult.Get(aec).
                            ToString()
            )
        },
```

```
                        new WriteLine{Text="Then send the result back
                                        to client"},
                        new SendReply{
                            Request=receive,
                            Content=new SendParametersContent{
                                Parameters={
                                    {"addResult",new
    InArgument<int>(addResult)},
                                },
                            },
                        },
                        new WriteLine{Text="sent result back done"}
                    },
                };
                service = new WorkflowService {
                    Name = "AddService",
                    Body = workflow
                };
                return service;
            }
        }
    }
```

3. **Add configuration code**:

   Open the App.config file and alter the configuration code as follows (create one if your project has no App.config file):

```xml
<?xml version="1.0" encoding="utf-8" ?>
<configuration>
  <system.serviceModel>
    <behaviors>
      <serviceBehaviors>
        <behavior>
          <serviceDebug includeExceptionDetailInFaults="True"
                        httpHelpPageEnabled="True"/>
          <serviceMetadata httpGetEnabled="True"/>
        </behavior>
      </serviceBehaviors>
    </behaviors>
  </system.serviceModel>
</configuration>
```

4. **Create workflow service host code**:

Set up the workflow host in the `Program.cs` file:

```
using System;
using System.Linq;
using System.Activities;
using System.Activities.Statements;
using System.ServiceModel.Activities;
namespace ReceiveAndReply {
    class Program {
        static void Main(string[] args) {
            ReceiveAndReplyWorkflow rrw =
                new ReceiveAndReplyWorkflow();
            WorkflowService wfService = rrw.GetInstance();
            Uri address =
                new Uri("http://localhost:8000/WFServices");
            WorkflowServiceHost host =
                new WorkflowServiceHost(wfService, address);
            try {
                Console.WriteLine("Opening Service...");
                host.Open();
                Console.WriteLine
                    ("WF service is listening on " + address.
                                                    ToString());
                Console.ReadLine();
            } catch (Exception e) {
                Console.WriteLine
                    ("some thing bad happened" + e.StackTrace);
            } finally {
                host.Close();
            }
        }
    }
}
```

5. **Run it:**

Set the `ReceiveAndReplyInCode` project as StartUp project and then press *Ctrl+F5* to run the project without debugging.

6. **Test it in WCF Test Client:**

Open WCF Test Client and add the service to the tool. Double-click `GetData()`, input two numbers , click the **Invoke** button, and we will get the result.

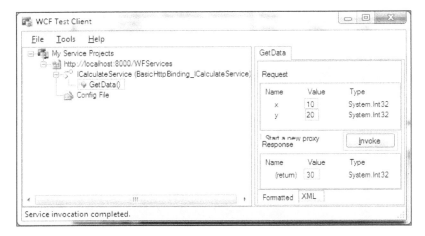

When we test it in the WCF Test Client, the server console will be updated as follows:

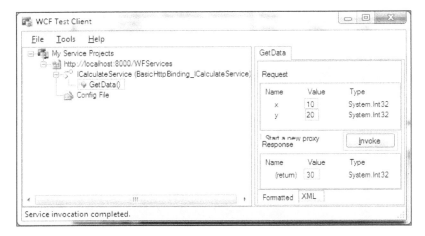

How it works...

▶ **Visual workflow or code workflow**:

In real applications, we should use visual workflow instead of code workflow. If we want to create workflow in imperative code, we have to take care of too many things; those are hidden in visual workflow. On the other hand, creating code workflow will help us understand workflow better. After all, all visual workflow declared as XAML will be compiled to .NET assembly before execution.

▶ **WorkflowService class**:

Let's again have a look at the code to see how it works. Consider this code line:

```
WorkflowService service;
```

One may wonder why we use `WorkflowService` class not Activity class. We use `WorkflowService` rather than Activity because `WorkflowService` enables us to run the workflow as a WCF service. By using `WorkflowService` class, we can configure and access the properties of a workflow service.

▶ **Receive activity and Send activity**:

We define WCF contract name, operation name, and parameters in the `Receive` activity. When we set `CanCreateInstance` property to `true`, every WCF request will create a new workflow instance to handle each request.

```
Receive receive = new Receive {
    ServiceContractName = "ICalculateService",
    OperationName = "Add",
    CanCreateInstance = true,
    Content = new ReceiveParametersContent {
        Parameters ={
            { "x",new OutArgument<int>(x) },
            { "y",new OutArgument<int>(y) }
        }
    }
};
```

Using the `SendReply` activity, the workflow service sends the result back to the client.

```
new SendReply{
    Request=receive,
    Content=new SendParametersContent{
        Parameters={
            { "addResult",new InArgument<int>(addResult) },
        },
    },
}
```

When the workflow is running, the client sends two integer numbers to the workflow, which adds the numbers and assigns the addition result to the `addResult` variable and then sends the `addResult` back to the client.

Sending and receiving a reply to a WCF message

In this task, we are going to create a WCF client workflow. The workflow will send a WCF request with two integer numbers to a WF service and receive a reply from the WCF service with the addition result.

Getting ready

For this task, we need to choose one of the previous tasks that we performed as the WF service—*Receiving and replying a WCF message* or *Receiving and replying to a WCF message in code workflow*. I will use the WF service that is hosted in IIS.

How to do it...

1. **Create a Workflow Console Application project**:

   Create a new Workflow Console Application named `SendAndReceive`.

2. **Find out service information**:

   Before moving to authoring a workflow service client, we need to find out some basic WCF service information—as we stated in the first task of this chapter, the famous ABC of WCF services.

   We can use WCF Test Client to collect those ABCs. Add WF service to WCF Test Client and double-click the `Config File`.

   ```
   <client>
       <endpoint address="http://localhost:8088/ReceiveAndReply/Service1.xamlx"
           binding="basicHttpBinding" bindingConfiguration="BasicHttpBinding_IService"
           contract="IService" name="BasicHttpBinding_IService" />
   </client>
   </system.serviceModel>
   </configuration>
   ```

Now, we find out the ABC of the workflow service:

- A(address): `http://localhost:8088/ReceiveAndReply/Service1.xamlx`

- B(binding): `basicHttpBinding`

- C(contract): `IService`

Besides the ABC information, we also need to find out the service parameters' names. Again, we can use WCF Test Client. Double-click `GetData()`, input two numbers, click the **Invoke** button, and we should get the service result. Now, click the XML table to see the string XML behind:

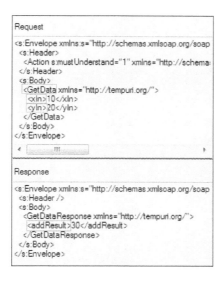

Now, we have the following:

- Operation name: `GetData`

- Request parameters' names: `xIn` and `yIn`

- Response parameter name: `addResult`

3. **Create a workflow**:

Open `Workflow1.xaml`, which is a workflow created by default, and perform the following actions:

   i.   Drag a `SendAndReceiveReply` activity to the designer panel.

   ii. Right-click the `Send` activity and select **Properties**.

   iii. Specify four properties of the `Send` activity. We obtained this information in step 2.

Make sure not to use double quotation marks (" ") around the `AddressUri` property.

   iv. Add an `Int32` type Variable named `result` to the **Sequence** scope:

Name	Variable type	Scope	Default
_handle1	CorrelationHandle	Sequence	*Handle cannot b*
result	Int32	Sequence	*Enter a VB expre:*

The `_handle1` variable is created by the `SendAndReceiveReply` activity automatically, and this variable will not be used in this task. Just leave it there.

v. Click the **Define...** link of the `Send` activity and input the operation parameters' names, which we obtained in step 2.

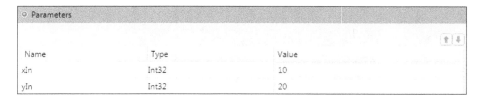

vi. Click the **Define...** link of the `ReceiveReplyForSend` activity and input the response parameter we obtained in step 2.

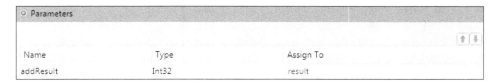

Please note that we must input exactly the same parameter name that we obtain from WCF Test Client.

vii. Add a `WriteLine` activity below the `ReceiveReplyForSend` activity and input `result.ToString()` in the text expression box. Now the workflow should look like the following screenshot:

4. **Run it**:

Save all files and set the `SendAndReceive` project as StartUp project. Press *Ctrl+F5* to run the workflow. We will see the following:

How it works...

The `Send` activity enables us to start a conversation with the WCF service. In the behind stage, the `Send` activity will fetch the `wsdl` file according to the endpoint address, and then generate a proxy that can be used to call the WCF service. So, the `Send` activity gets many tedious things done and we can use the activity by just performing some configurations.

We can use a `Send` activity alone to send a message without expecting a response, or we can use a `Send` activity paired with a `Receive` activity to send a message and wait till a response is received from the service.

In this task, we use the second pattern by dragging the built-in `SendAndReceiveReply` pattern to the designer panel.

There's more

We can also add the WF service to the project service reference and use the service like a local activity. We can accomplish it by following the next steps:

1. Add a WF service to the project's service reference.

2. Build the project.
3. Now we can see the WF service operation appearing in the toolbox.

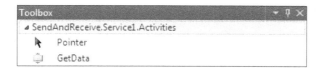

4. Use the `GetData` activity just like a local activity.

5. Edit the properties of the `GetData` activity:

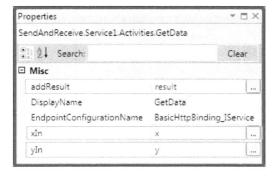

6. Save the workflow and build the project.

It is easy to consume a WF service like this; however, there are two drawbacks as follows:

▶ Visual Studio 2010 is needed, which is not available in the customized WF designer by default.

▶ We have to add a service reference to the project. While many workflows exist in XAML files and may even be stored in a database, adding references is not an option for standalone workflows.

Sending and receiving a reply to a WCF message in code workflow

In this task, we are going to create a WCF client workflow. The workflow will send a WCF request with two integer numbers to a WF service and receive a reply from a WCF service with the addition result.

Getting ready

Now that we have finished at least one of the previous tasks—*Receiving and replying to a WCF message* or *Receiving and replying to a WCF message in code workflow*—we can choose one of them as the WF service in this task. In this task I will use the code-style WF service.

How to do it...

1. **Create a Workflow Console Application project**:

   Create a new Workflow Console project and name it `SendAndReceiveInCode`.

2. **Create workflow in imperative code**:

   Add a new class file `SendAndReceiveWorkflow.cs` to the project and fill the file with the following code:

```
using System;
using System.Activities;
using System.ServiceModel;
using System.ServiceModel.Activities;
using System.Activities.Statements;
namespace SendAndReceive {
    class SendAndReceiveWorkflow {
        public Activity GetInstance() {
            Variable<int> x = new Variable<int>("x", 10);
            Variable<int> y = new Variable<int>("y", 20);
```

```
            Variable<int> addResult = new
Variable<int>("addResult", 0);
            var endpoint = new System.ServiceModel.Endpoint {
                AddressUri = new Uri("http://localhost:8000/
WFServices"),
                Binding = new BasicHttpBinding(),
            };
            Send addRequest = new Send {
                ServiceContractName="ICalculateService",
                Endpoint = endpoint,
                OperationName = "GetData",
                Content = new SendParametersContent {
                    Parameters = {
                        {"xIn",new InArgument<int>(x)},
                        {"yIn",new InArgument<int>(y)}
                    },
                },
            };
            var workflow = new CorrelationScope {
                Body = new Sequence {
                    Variables = { x, y, addResult },
                    Activities ={
                        new WriteLine{Text="Send x:10 and y:20 to
                                    WF service"},
                        addRequest,
                        new ReceiveReply{
                            Request=addRequest,
                            Content=new ReceiveParametersContent{
                                Parameters={
                                    {"addResult",new
OutArgument<int>(addResult)}
                                }
                            },
                        },
                        new WriteLine{
                            Text=new InArgument<string>(
                                aec=>(
                                    "The result is:"+addResult.
Get(aec).ToString()
                                )
                            )
                        }
```

```
                }
            }
        };
        return workflow;
    }
  }
}
```

3. **Create workflow host code**:

Open the `Program.cs` file and alter the present code to:

```
using System.Activities;
namespace SendAndReceive {
    class Program {
        static void Main(string[] args) {
            SendAndReceiveWorkflow srw =
                new SendAndReceiveWorkflow();
            WorkflowInvoker.Invoke(srw.GetInstance());
        }
    }
}
```

4. **Run it**:

Follow the steps given next:

i. Set the `ReceiveAndReplyInCode` project (the project we created in the task *Receiving and replying WCF message in code workflow*) as StartUp project and press *Ctrl+F5* to run the service.

ii. Set the `SendAndReceiveInCode` project as StartUp project and press *Ctrl+F5* to run the WF service's caller workflow (client).

The `ReceiveAndReplyInCode` Console looks like this:

The `SendAndReceiveInCode` Console looks like this:

How it works...

In this task, there are three important activities we need to focus on.

▸ **Send activity**:

The following code creates a WCF endpoint to which the `Send` activity will send messages. In the endpoint object, we specify the A (address) of a WCF service as `http://localhost:8000/WFServices` and the B (binding) as `BasicHttpBinding`.

```
var endpoint = new System.ServiceModel.Endpoint {
    AddressUri = new Uri("http://localhost:8000/WFServices"),
    Binding = new BasicHttpBinding(),
};
```

The next code creates a `Send` activity. Please note that the `Send` activity will generate a WCF contract dynamically when it is running.

```
Send addRequest = new Send {
    ServiceContractName="ICalculateService",
        Endpoint = endpoint,
        OperationName = "GetData",
        Content = new SendParametersContent {
        Parameters = {
            {"x",new InArgument<int>(x)},
            {"y",new InArgument<int>(y)}
        },
    },
};
```

In the `Send` activity, we specify C (contract name), which we defined in the WF service, along with operation name and parameters. By using these properties, the `Send` activity is able to establish a "connection" (not always connected) with WF service.

▶ **ReceiveReply activity:**

We can receive messages from the WF service by using a `ReceiveReply` activity.

```
new ReceiveReply{
    Request=addRequest,
    Content=new ReceiveParametersContent{
        Parameters={
            {"addResult",new OutArgument<int>(addResult)}
        }
    }
}
```

The `ReceiveActivity` will receive the WCF response message and will assign the value to the `addResult` Variable.

▶ **CorrelationScope:**

If we have many `Send` activities and `ReceiveReply` activities in one workflow, we have to pay particular attention to the `CorrelationScope` activity. By using `CorrelationScope`, we can make a `Send` activity pair with a `ReceiveReply` activity. Every `ReceiveReply` activity will receive messages initiated by a `Send` activity in the same correlation scope.

Using CancellationScope activity

As we know, the Parallel activity will not finish execution until all of its child branches have finished execution. Sometimes, we want to break the parallel if one of its branch finishes execution and cancel the other branches. To do this, we can use a `CancellationScope` activity. In this task, we want to order products from two dealers (Dealer A and Dealer B) at the same time. In this situation, the two dealers are in a competition, and so the one who ships the product faster wins the business.

How to do it...

1. **Create a Workflow Console Application:**

   Create a new Workflow Console Application project and name it `UseCancellationScope`.

2. **Create a code workflow file:**

   Add to the project a new class file and name it `WorkflowWithCancellationScope.cs`. Fill the file with the following code:

   ```
   using System.Activities;
   using System.Activities.Statements;
   ```

```
using System;
namespace UseCancellationScope {
    class WorkflowWithCancellationScope {
        public Activity GetInstance() {
            Activity workflow = new System.Activities.Statements.
Parallel {
                CompletionCondition = true,
                Branches ={
                    new CancellationScope{
                        Body=new Sequence{
                            Activities={
                                new Delay{
                                    Duration=new
InArgument<TimeSpan>(TimeSpan.FromSeconds(6))
                                },
                                new WriteLine{Text="Dealer A:Your
product has been shipped"}
                            },
                        },
                        CancellationHandler=new
WriteLine{Text="Dealer A,cancel my order."}
                    },
                    new CancellationScope{
                        Body=new Sequence{
                            Activities={
                                new Delay{
                                    Duration=new
InArgument<TimeSpan>(TimeSpan.FromSeconds(5))
                                },
                                new WriteLine{Text="Dealer B:Your
product has been shipped"}
                            }
                        },
                        CancellationHandler=new
WriteLine{Text="Dealer B,cancel my order"}
                    }
                }
            };
            return workflow;
        }
    }
}
```

3. **Create workflow host code**:

Open the `Program.cs` file and alter the code to:

```
using System;
using System.Activities;
using System.Activities.Statements;
namespace UseCancellationScope {
    class Program {
        static void Main(string[] args) {
            WorkflowWithCancellationScope wcs =
                new WorkflowWithCancellationScope();
            WorkflowInvoker.Invoke(wcs.GetInstance());
        }
    }
}
```

4. **Run it**:

Press *Ctrl+F5* to build and run the workflow without debugging. Because dealer A uses 6 seconds to ship the product to us, whereas dealer B uses only 5 seconds, we will see the following result:

How it works...

This workflow is simply a `Parallel` activity with two `CancellationScope` activities. By default, a `Parallel` activity will finish executing once all of its child branches have finished executing. While in this task, we set `CompletionCondition` to `true` so that the `Parallel` will finish if one of its branch runs to its end.

We created two `CancellationScope` activities as the `Parallel` activity's branches and assigned each `CancellationHandler` with a `WriteLine` activity:

```
CancellationHandler=new WriteLine{Text="Dealer A,cancel my order."}
```

When the workflow is running, the second `CancellationScope` (dealer B) finishes in 5 seconds, whereupon the first `CancellationHandler` (dealer A) is executed to inform dealer A that the order given to him is cancelled.

There's more

To use the CancellationScope activity in visual workflow, please follow these steps:

1. Drag a Parallel activity to the workflow designer panel. Right-click the activity and select **Properties**. Set the ConpletionCondition property to True:

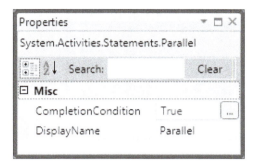

2. Drag two CancellationScope activities into the Parallel activity.

3. Drag two Sequence activities to the bodies of the two CancellationScope activities respectively.

4. Drag two Delay activities to the two Sequence activities respectively. Set the left Delay activity's delay time to 6 seconds and set the right Delay activity's delay time to 5 seconds.

5. Add two WriteLine activities below the Delay activities respectively. Input string **"DealerA: Your product has been shipped."** to the left WriteLine activity and **"DealerB: Your product has been shipped."** to the right-hand Writeline activity.

6. Add two WriteLine activities to the two CancelationHandler activities. Input string **"DealerA, cancel my order"** to the left WriteLine activity and input string **"DealerB, cancel my order"** to the right Writeline activity.

The final workflow should be as shown in the following screenshot:

Performing a transaction by using TransactionScope activity

In this task, we will create a workflow with `TransactionScope` activity, in which a customized activity will insert some data in the database. If any exception/error occurs, the newly inserted data will be rolled back.

How to do it...

1. **Create a Workflow Console Application**:

   Create a new Workflow Console Application and name it `UseTransactionScope`.

2. **Create a database for testing**:

   Create a new database in SQL Server (or SQL Server Express) and name it `TransactionDB`. Use the following SQL statement to create a new table:

   ```
   create table UserTable(
         UserID nvarchar(50) primary key
   )
   ```

3. **Add references to the project:**

   Add a reference to the `System.Tranactions` namespace because we are going to use `IsolationLevel` enumeration in our code.

4. **Create** `InsertDataToDBActivity` **code:**

   Add a new class file to the project and name it `InsertDataToDBActivity.cs`. By using this activity, we can insert a row of data into the database that has been created in advance. Fill the file with the following code. Replace the SQL Server connection string with our own one.

```
using System;
using System.Activities;
using System.Data.SqlClient;
namespace UseTransactionScope {
    public class InsertDataToDBActivity : NativeActivity {
        public InArgument<string> UserID { get; set; }
        protected override void Execute(NativeActivityContext
context) {
            SqlConnection con = new System.Data.SqlClient.
SqlConnection();
            con.ConnectionString =
                "Data Source=(local);Initial Catalog=TransactionDB
;Integrated Security=True";
            con.Open();
            SqlCommand cmd = con.CreateCommand();
            cmd.CommandText =
                string.Format("insert into UserTable (UserID)
values ('{0}')", UserID.Get(context));
            cmd.ExecuteNonQuery();
            con.Close();
        }
    }
}
```

5. **Create workflow code:**

   Add a new class file in the project and name it `TransactionWorkflow.cs`. The class will define the workflow structure. Fill the file with the following code:

```
using System;
using System.Activities;
using System.Activities.Statements;
namespace UseTransactionScope {
    class TransactionWorkflow {
        public Activity GetInstance() {
```

```
Variable<int> num1 = new Variable<int>("num1", 0);
Variable<int> num2 = new Variable<int>("num2", 10);
Variable<double> result = new
Variable<double>("result");
Activity workflow = new Sequence {
    Variables = { num1, num2, result },
    Activities = {
        new WriteLine{Text="Transaction workflow is
                        running…"},
        new TransactionScope{
            IsolationLevel=System.Transactions.
IsolationLevel.Serializable,
                AbortInstanceOnTransactionFailure=false,
                Body=new Sequence{
                    Activities={
                        new WriteLine{Text="Begin
                                    Transaction"},
                        new InsertDataToDBActivity(){
UserID=Guid.NewGuid().ToString()
                        },
                        new WriteLine{Text="data inserted
                                    to database "},
                        new Assign<double>{
                            To=result,
                            Value=new
InArgument<double>(aec=>(num2.Get(aec)/num1.Get(aec))),
                        },
                        new WriteLine{Text="End
                                    Transaction"}
                    }
                },
            }
        }
    };
    return workflow;
}
}
}
```

6. **Create workflow host code**:

   Open the `Program.cs` file and alter the code to:

   ```
   using System;
   ```

```
using System.Activities;
using System.Activities.Statements;
using System.Threading;
namespace UseTransactionScope {
    class Program {
        static void Main(string[] args) {
            TransactionWorkflow tw = new TransactionWorkflow();
            AutoResetEvent waitHandler = new
AutoResetEvent(false);
            WorkflowApplication wfApp = new
WorkflowApplication(tw.GetInstance());
            wfApp.OnUnhandledException = (arg) => {
Console.WriteLine(arg.UnhandledException.Message);
                return UnhandledExceptionAction.Terminate;
            };
            wfApp.Completed = (arg) => {
                waitHandler.Set();
            };
            wfApp.Run();
            waitHandler.WaitOne();
        }
    }
}
```

7. **Run it**:

Press *Ctrl+F5* to run the project. By default, we will see the following:

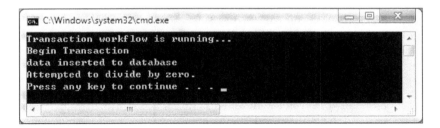

If we open the database table, we will find no data has been inserted into the table. Next, we have to change the workflow definition (`TransactionWorkflow.cs`) from:

```
Variable<int> num1 = new Variable<int>("num1", 0);
```

to:

```
Variable<int> num1 = new Variable<int>("num1", 1);
```

This is to ensure that the divided-by-zero exception will not occur any more. Press *Ctrl+F5 and* we will see the following:

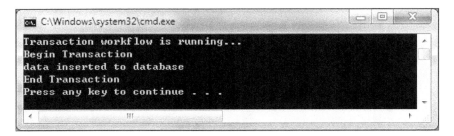

How it works...

Let's start from the `Program.cs` file:

```
wfApp.OnUnhandledException = (arg) => {
    Console.WriteLine("Attempted to divide by zero exception, database
rolled back.");
    return UnhandledExceptionAction.Terminate;
};
```

By using this code block, any unhandled exception generated by the workflow will be handled here. In our workflow, the divided-by-zero exception will be handled here. Once an exception occurs, workflow will be terminated and the database rolled back. Be aware of the fact that the table will be locked during the transaction processing. This is because we specified the following in the `TransactionScope` activity:

```
IsolationLevel=System.Transactions.IsolationLevel.Serializable
```

By doing this, the database will place locks on all data that is used in a transaction, and will prevent other users from updating and making non-repeatable reads.

There's more

To use Transaction Scope Activity in visual workflow, open `Workflow1.xaml`, which is created by default. Then we need to create a workflow as shown in the following screenshot:

Please note that if we cannot find the `InsertDataToDBActivity` activity, we need to rebuild the project by pressing *F6*.

Performing compensation by using Compensable activity

Imagine a scenario where we are buying a computer online and money has been deducted from our bank account. Suddenly an unexpected exception occurs, workflow stops, and the purchase gets cancelled. Obviously, such a thing should not happen in real life. If an exception occurs that induces workflow stop, the money should be returned back to our account. In WF4 we can use a `Compensable` activity to handle such a compensation job.

How to do it...

1. **Create a Workflow Console Application project**:

   Create a new Workflow Console application project and name it `UseCompensableActivity`.

2. **Create workflow code**:

   Add a new class file to the project and name it `CompensationWokflow.cs`. Fill the file with the following code:

```csharp
using System;
using System.Activities;
using System.Activities.Statements;
namespace UseCompensableActivity {
    class CompensationWorkflow {
        public Activity GetInstance() {
            Variable<int> num1 = new Variable<int>("num1", 10);
            Variable<int> num2 = new Variable<int>("num2", 0);
            Variable<int> result = new Variable<int>();
            Activity workflow = new Sequence {
                Variables = { num1, num2, result },
                Activities = {
                    new CompensableActivity{
                        Body=new WriteLine{Text="compensable
                                        activity take action"},
                        CompensationHandler=
                            new WriteLine{Text="CompensationHandler
                                        do some work..."}
                    },
                    new Assign{// This activity will generate a
divided by zero exception.
                        To=new OutArgument<int>(result),
                        Value=new InArgument<int>(aec=>(num1.
Get(aec)/num2.Get(aec))),
                    }
                },
            };
            return workflow;
        }
    }
}
```

3. **Create workflow host code**:

Open the `Program.cs` file and alter the code to:

```
using System;
using System.Activities;
using System.Activities.Statements;
using System.Threading;
namespace UseCompensableActivity {
    class Program {
        static void Main(string[] args) {
            CompensationWorkflow cw = new CompensationWorkflow();
            AutoResetEvent waitHandler = new
AutoResetEvent(false);
            WorkflowApplication wfApp = new
WorkflowApplication(cw.GetInstance());
            wfApp.OnUnhandledException = (arg) => {
                return UnhandledExceptionAction.Cancel;
            };
            wfApp.Completed = (arg) => {
                waitHandler.Set();
            };
            wfApp.Run();
            waitHandler.WaitOne();
        }
    }
}
```

4. **Run it**:

Press *Ctrl+F5* to run the workflow. We should see this:

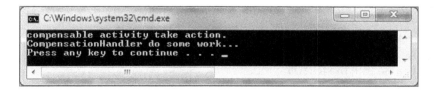

How it works...

As soon as the workflow starts, the `Writeline` activity in the body of `CompensableActivity` performs its action and prints its message to the control.

```
new CompensableActivity{
    Body=new WriteLine{Text="compensable activity take action."},
```

```
        CompensationHandler=
            new WriteLine{Text="CompensationHandler do some work..."}
    },
```

`CompensationHandler` will not be executed at this time. Next, the `Assign` activity will generate a divided-by-zero exception due to the setting of `0` as the value of the Variable `num2`.

```
new Assign{
    To=new OutArgument<int>(result),
    Value=new
        InArgument<int>(aec=>(num1.Get(aec)/num2.Get(aec))),
}
```

The exception will be captured (code in `Program.cs`) and the workflow cancelled.

```
wfApp.OnUnhandledException = (arg) => {
    return UnhandledExceptionAction.Cancel;
};
```

Before the workflow is fully terminated, `CompensationHandler` will be executed and do some compensation work.

Performing manual compensation by using Compensate activity

In a certain workflow execution phase, we may want to compensate an activity manually (rather than driven by an exception/error)—a `Compensate` activity will handle this job.

How to do it...

1. **Create a Workflow Console Application project**:

    Create a new Workflow Console Application and name it `UseCompensateActivity`.

2. **Create workflow code**:

    Add a new class file to the project and name it `CompensationWorkflow.cs`.
    Fill the file with the following code:

    ```
    using System;
    using System.Activities;
    using System.Activities.Statements;
    namespace UseCompensateActivity {
        class CompensationWorkflow {
            public Activity GetInstance() {
                Variable<CompensationToken> token=new
    Variable<CompensationToken>();
    ```

```
                Activity workflow = new Sequence() {
                    Variables={token},
                    Activities = {
                        new CompensableActivity{
                            Body=new WriteLine{Text="Compensableactivity
                                            body take action."},
                            CompensationHandler=new WriteLine{Text="Co
mpensationHandler do compensation work."},
                            Result=token
                        },
                        new WriteLine{Text="Do some other work after
                                    CompensableActivity."},
                        new Compensate{
                            Target=token
                        }
                    }
                };
                return workflow;
            }
        }
    }
```

3. **Create host code**:

   Open the `Program.cs` file and alter code to:

```
using System;
using System.Activities;
using System.Activities.Statements;
namespace UseCompensateActivity {
    class Program {
        static void Main(string[] args) {
            CompensationWorkflow cw=new CompensationWorkflow();
            WorkflowInvoker.Invoke(cw.GetInstance());
        }
    }
}
```

4. **Run it**:

Press *Ctrl+F5* to run the workflow and you should see the following:

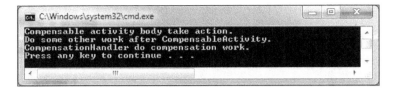

How it works...

How could a compensate activity know which `CompensableActivity` it is going to compensate? We use `CompensationToken` to link them together.

```
Variable<CompensationToken> token=new Variable<CompensationToken>();
```

In `CompensableActivity`, we assign the token to the `Result` property.

```
new CompensableActivity{
    Body=new WriteLine{Text="Compensable activity body take action."},
    CompensationHandler=new WriteLine{Text="CompensationHandler do
compensation work."},
    Result=token
},
```

In the `Compensate` activity we assign token to the `Target` property:

```
new Compensate{
    Target=token
}
```

If there is more than one `CompensableActivity` activity in the workflow, the token will link to the latest assigned one.

Performing confirmation by using Confirm activity

Like performing compensation, we can also perform confirmation by explicitly using a `Confirm` activity. Confirmation will also be triggered when workflow is successfully finished.

How to do it...

1. **Create a Workflow Console Application project**:

   Create a new Workflow Console Application project and name it `UseConfirmActivity`.

2. **Create workflow code**:

   Add a new class file to the project and name it `ConfirmationWorkflow.cs`. Then fill the file with the following code:

```
using System;
using System.Activities;
using System.Activities.Statements;
namespace UseConfirmActivity {
    class ConfirmationWorkflow {
        public Activity GetInstance() {
            Variable<CompensationToken> token = new
Variable<CompensationToken>();
            Activity workflow = new Sequence() {
                Variables = { token },
                Activities = {
                    new CompensableActivity{
                      Body=new WriteLine{Text="CompensableActivity1
                                      body take action."},
                        ConfirmationHandler=new WriteLine{Text="Co
mpensableActivity1 confirmed."},

                    },
                    new CompensableActivity{
                      Body=new WriteLine{Text="CompensableActivity2
                                      body take action."},
                        ConfirmationHandler=new WriteLine{Text=
                            "CompensableActivity2 confirmed."},
                        Result=token
                    },
                    new Confirm{
                        Target=token
                    }
                }
            };
            return workflow;
        }
    }
}
```

3. **Create workflow host code**:

Open the `Program.cs` file and alter the code to:

```
using System;
using System.Activities;
using System.Activities.Statements;
namespace UseConfirmActivity {
    class Program {
        static void Main(string[] args) {
            ConfirmationWorkflow cw = new ConfirmationWorkflow();
            WorkflowInvoker.Invoke(cw.GetInstance());
        }
    }
}
```

4. **Run it**:

Press *Ctrl+F5* to run the workflow and we should see this:

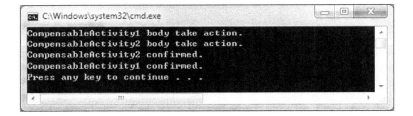

How it works...

If we have a careful look at the result, we shall see that `compensableActivity1` and `compensableActivity2` execute one after the other, and then the confirm activity executes as the confirm activity is linked to `CompensableActivity2` by token. The `ConfirmationHandler` executes and prints a line of message to the console.

When the workflow finishes successfully, the `ConfirmationHandler` of `CompensableActivity1` will take action automatically and print a line of message to the console.

4
Manipulating Collections

In this chapter, we will cover:

- ▶ Printing collection items
- ▶ Using AddToCollection<T> activity
- ▶ Using ClearCollection<T> activity
- ▶ Using RemoveFromCollection<T> activity
- ▶ Using ExistsInCollection<T> activity

Introduction

Imagine that we have defined a `List<T>` type Variable in workflow, and we want to add, remove, and update items of the collection object. By default, WF4 provides us with four activities—`AddToCollection<T>`, `ClearCollection<T>`, `RemoveFromCollection<T>`, and `ExistsInCollection<T>`—using which we can manipulate collection as we wish.

Printing collection items

In this task, we will customize an activity that can print all collection items to Console Application.

How to do it

1. **Create a Workflow Console Application**:

   Create a new Workflow Console Application and name it
   `PrintingCollectionItems`.

2. **Create an Activity that can print collection items to the Windows Console**:

   Add a new **Code Activity** to the project and name it `CollectionPrinter.cs`.
   Refer to the following screenshot:

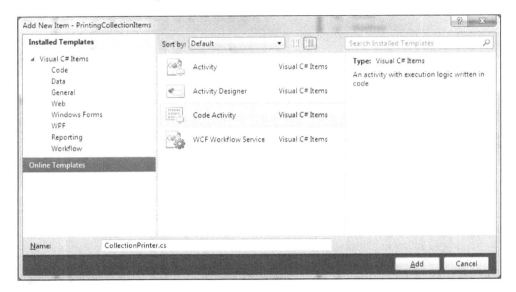

   Open the `CollectionPrinter.cs` file and alter the code as follows:

```
using System;
using System.Collections.Generic;
using System.Activities;
namespace PrintingCollectionItems {
    public sealed class CollectionPrinter<T> : CodeActivity {
        public InArgument<ICollection<T>> CollectionInArg { get;
set; }
        protected override void Execute(CodeActivityContext
context) {
            ICollection<T> collection = CollectionInArg.
Get<ICollection<T>>(context);
            if (collection.Count > 0) {
                Console.WriteLine("---Print Collection Start---");
```

```
        foreach (var item in collection) {
            Console.WriteLine(item.ToString());
        }
        Console.WriteLine("---Print Collection End---");
    } else {
        Console.WriteLine("Collection is empty.");
    }
  }
 }
}
```

3. **Build the project**:

   Build the project so that the custom activity will appear in the toolbox.

4. **Create a visual workflow**:

   To create visual workflow, we need to perform the following actions:

   i.   Open the default created workflow file `Workflow1.xaml`. Drag a **Sequence** activity to the design panel.

   ii. Drag a **CollectionPrinterActivity** activity onto the Sequence activity. A dialog box will appear asking us to choose type; here we choose **String**.

   iii. Click the **Imports** button and type in `System.Collection.ObjectModel` to imported the namespace `System.Collections.ObjectModel` to this workflow.

iv. Create an `ICollection<String>` type Variable `people` for this workflow and assign its default value with this VB Expression:

```
New Collection(Of String) From {"Steven", "Andrew", "Jophy"}
```

v. Assign the variable `people` to the `CollectionInArg` property of `CollectionPrinterActivity`.

The following is the final workflow:

5. **Run it**:

Set `PrintingCollectionItems` as StartUp project. Press *Ctrl+F5* to run the project; we will see the following:

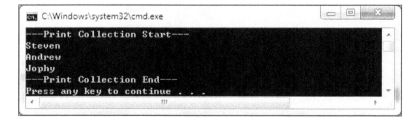

How it works...

In this task, we created an activity that can accept generic type Collection object. We will use this activity throughout this chapter. We need to make sure we have finished this task before moving ahead.

There's more

We can also use `CollectionPrinterActivity` in code-style workflow. To create a corresponding workflow in code, open the `Program.cs` file and alter the code to:

```
using System;
using System.Activities;
using System.Activities.Statements;
using System.Collections.Generic;
using System.Activities.Expressions;
namespace PrintingCollectionItems {
    class Program {
        static void Main(string[] args) {
            //WorkflowInvoker.Invoke(new Workflow1());
            WorkflowInvoker.Invoke(GetWfInstance());
        }
        static Activity GetWfInstance() {
            Variable<ICollection<String>> people = new
Variable<ICollection<string>>() {
                Default = new LambdaValue<ICollection<String>>(
                    ctx => new List<String> { "Steven",
"Andrew","Jophy" }
                    ),
            };
            Activity workflow = new Sequence() {
                Variables = { people },
                Activities = {
                    new CollectionPrinter<String>(){
                        CollectionInArg=people
                    }
                },
            };
            return workflow;
        }
    }
}
```

Uncomment the following to run XAML-style workflow:

```
//WorkflowInvoker.Invoke(new Workflow1());
```

Using AddToCollection<T> activity

In this task, we will use the AddToCollection<T> activity to add items to a collection object.

Getting ready...

We need to make sure we have finished the task of *Printing collection items* for us to be able to use the CollectionPrinterActivity activity in this task.

How to do it...

1. **Create a Console Workflow Application**:

   Create a new Workflow Console Application and name it UsingAddToCollectionActivity.

2. **Create a visual workflow**:

   We need to perform the following actions:

   i. Open the Workflow1.xaml file that is created by default. Click the **Imports** button and type in System.Collections.ObjectModel to import the System.Collections.ObjectModel namespace to this workflow.

   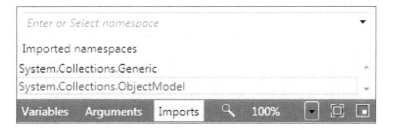

   ii. Drag a Sequence activity to the workflow designer and then drag an AddToCollection activity onto the Sequence activity. Next, drag the customized CollectionPrinter activity right below the AddToCollection—the type is String. Add a new ICollection<String> variable named people to the Sequence's scope. We can see the workflow shown in the following screenshot:

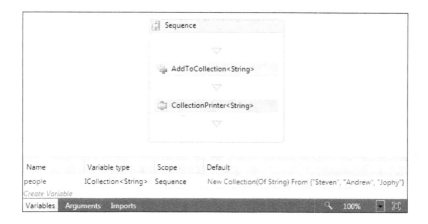

iii. Set the properties of the `AddToCollection<String>` activity as shown in the following screenshot:

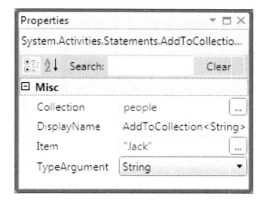

iv. Set the properties of the `CollectionPrinter<String>` activity:

3. Set `UsingAddToCollectionActivity` as StartUp project and press *Ctrl+F5* to run the project. We will see:

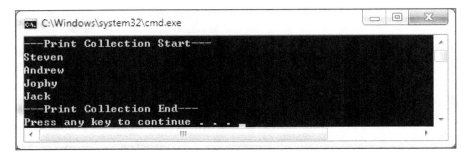

How it works...

The `AddToCollection<T>` activity will append the new item to the end of the collection object. If we want to insert an item to a specified position, we may need to create our own activity to do this.

There's more

We can also use the `AddToCollection<T>` activity in code-style workflow. To use `AddToCollection<T>` in code workflow, open the `Program.cs` file and alter the code to:

```
using System;
using System.Activities;
using System.Activities.Statements;
using System.Collections.Generic;
using System.Activities.Expressions;
using PrintingCollectionItems;
namespace UsingAddToCollectionActivity {
    class Program {
        static void Main(string[] args) {
            //WorkflowInvoker.Invoke(new Workflow1());
            WorkflowInvoker.Invoke(GetWFInstance());
        }
        static Activity GetWFInstance() {
            Variable<ICollection<String>> people = new
Variable<ICollection<string>>() {
                Default = new LambdaValue<ICollection<String>>(
                    ctx => new List<String> { "Steven", "Andrew",
                                              "Jophy" }
                ),
            };
```

```
Activity workflow = new Sequence() {
    Variables = { people },
    Activities = {
        new AddToCollection<String>(){
            Collection=people,
            Item="Jack"
        },
        new CollectionPrinter<String>{
            CollectionInArg=people
        }
    }
};
return workflow;
    }
  }
}
```

Uncomment the following to run XAML-style workflow:

```
//WorkflowInvoker.Invoke(new Workflow1());
```

Using ClearCollection<T> activity

In this task, we will use the `ClearCollection<T>` activity to clear the content of a collection object.

Getting ready

We need to make sure we have finished the task of *Printing collection items* for us to be able to use the `CollectionPrinter` activity in this task.

How to do it...

1. **Create a Workflow Console Application**:

   Create a new Workflow Console Application and name it `UsingClearCollectionActivity`.

2. **Create a visual workflow**:

Perform the following steps in order to create a visual workflow:

i. Open `Workflow1.xaml`, which is the workflow created by default. Click the **Imports** button and type in `System.Collections.ObjectModel` to import the `System.Collections.ObjectModel` namespace to this workflow.

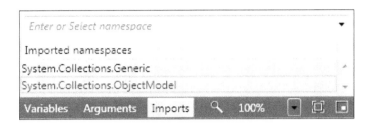

ii. Drag a Sequence activity to the workflow designer and then drag a `CollectionPrinter` activity to the designer panel two times to add two `CollectionPrinter<String>` activities to the designer panel. Next, drag a `ClearCollection` activity between the two `CollectionPinter` activities—the type is `String`. Add a new `ICollection<String>` variable named `people` to the Sequence's scope. We can see the workflow as shown in the following screenshot:

iii. Set the properties of both the `CollectionPrinter<String>` activities:

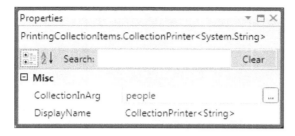

iv. Set the properties for the `ClearCollection<String>` activity:

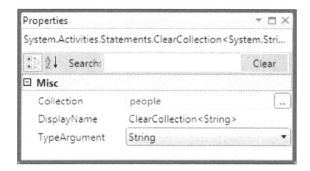

3. **Run it:**

Set `UsingClearCollectionActivity` as StartUp project, and then press *Ctrl+F5* to run the project. We will see the following:

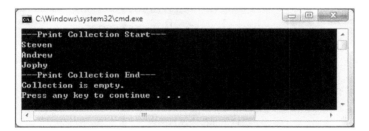

How it works...

By using this activity, we can remove all collection items, so that we can reuse the collection variable again rather than defining a new one.

There's more

We can also use the `ClearCollection<T>` activity in code workflow. Open the
`program.cs` file and alter the code to:

```
using System;
using System.Activities;
using System.Activities.Statements;
using System.Collections.Generic;
using System.Activities.Expressions;
using PrintingCollectionItems;
namespace UsingClearCollectionActivity {
    class Program {
        static void Main(string[] args) {
            //WorkflowInvoker.Invoke(new Workflow1());
            WorkflowInvoker.Invoke(GetWFInstance());
        }
        static Activity GetWFInstance() {
            Variable<ICollection<String>> people =
                    new Variable<ICollection<string>>() {
                Default = new LambdaValue<ICollection<String>>(
                    ctx => new List<String> { "Steven", "Andrew",
                                                     "Jophy" }
                ),
            };
            Activity workflow = new Sequence() {
                Variables = { people },
                Activities = {
                    new CollectionPrinter<String>{
                        CollectionInArg=people
                    },
                    new ClearCollection<String>(){
                        Collection=people
                    },
                    new CollectionPrinter<String>{
                        CollectionInArg=people
                    }
                }
            };
            return workflow;
        }
    }
}
```

Uncomment the following to run XAML-style workflow:

```
//WorkflowInvoker.Invoke(new Workflow1());
```

Using RemoveFromCollection<T> activity

In this task, we will use the `RemoveFromCollection<T>` activity to remove an item from a collection object.

Getting ready

We need to make sure we have finished the task of *Printing collection items* for us to be able to use the `CollectionPrinterActivity` in this task.

How to do it...

1. **Create a Console Workflow Application:**

    Create a new Workflow Console Application, and name it `UsingRemoveFromCollectionActivity`.

2. **Create a workflow**:

    We need to perform the following tasks to create a workflow:

    i. Open `Workflow1.xaml`, which is the workflow created by default. Click the **Imports** button and type in `System.Collections.ObjectModel` to import the `System.Collections.ObjectModel` namespace to this workflow.

ii. Drag a Sequence activity to the workflow designer panel. Next, drag
     `CollectionPrinter` activity to the designer panel two times. Now drag a
     `RemoveFromCollection` activity between the two `CollectionPinter`
     activities—the type is `String`. Add a new `ICollection<String>` variable
     named `people` to the Sequence's scope. We can see the workflow as shown
     in the following screenshot:

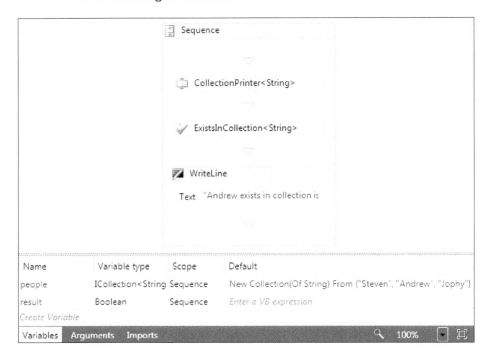

iii. Set the properties of both the `CollectionPrinter<String>` activities:

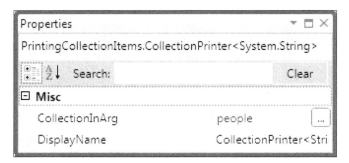

iv. Set the properties of the `RemoveFromCollection<String>` activity:

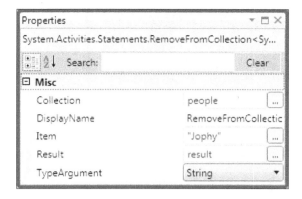

3. **Run it**:

    Set `UsingRemoveFromCollectionActivity` as StartUp project and press *Ctrl+F5* to run the project. We will see the following:

How it works...

The `Result` property of `RemoveFromCollection<String>` activity indicates whether or not an item is deleted successfully. If the item exists and is deleted by this activity, then the `Result` property will be assigned a `True` value.

There's more

To use the `RemoveFromCollection<T>` activity in code-style workflow, open the `Program.cs` file and alter the code to:

```
using System;
using System.Activities;
using System.Activities.Statements;
using System.Collections.Generic;
using System.Activities.Expressions;
```

```
using PrintingCollectionItems;
namespace UsingRemoveFromCollectionActivity {
    class Program {
        static void Main(string[] args) {
            //WorkflowInvoker.Invoke(new Workflow1());
            WorkflowInvoker.Invoke(GetWFInstance());
        }
        static Activity GetWFInstance() {
            Variable<ICollection<String>> people =
                    new Variable<ICollection<string>>() {
                Default = new LambdaValue<ICollection<String>>(
                    ctx => new List<String> { "Steven", "Andrew",
                                                "Jophy" }
                ),
            };
            Variable<Boolean> result = new Variable<bool>();
            Activity workflow = new Sequence() {
                Variables = { people,result },
                Activities = {
                    new CollectionPrinter<String>{
                        CollectionInArg=people
                    },
                    new RemoveFromCollection<String>(){
                        Collection=people,
                        Item="Jophy",
                        Result=result,
                    },
                    new CollectionPrinter<String>{
                        CollectionInArg=people
                    }
                }
            };
            return workflow;
        }
    }
}
```

Uncomment the following to run XAML-style workflow:

```
//WorkflowInvoker.Invoke(new Workflow1());
```

Using ExistsInCollection<T> activity

In this task, we will use the `ExistsInCollection<T>` activity to check whether or not a specified item exists in the collection object.

Getting ready

We need to make sure we have finished the task of *Printing collection items* for us to be able to use `CollectionPrinterActivity` in this task.

How to do it...

1. **Create a Console Workflow Application**:

   Create a new Workflow Console Application and name it `UsingExistsInCollectionActivity`.

2. **Create a workflow**:

   We need to perform the following actions to create a workflow:

   i. Open `Workflow1.xaml`, which is the workflow created by default. Click the **Imports** button and type in `System.Collections.ObjectModel` to import the `System.Collections.ObjectModel` namespace to this workflow.

   ii. Drag a Sequence activity into the designer panel. Next, drag an `ExistsInCollection` activity right below the `CollectionPrinter` activity—the type is `String`. Now drag a `WriteLine` activity below the `ExistsCollection` activity. Add a new `ICollection<String>` variable named `people` to the Sequence's scope. Add a `Boolean` type variable `result` to the Sequence's scope.

We can see the workflow as shown in the following screenshot:

iii. Set the propertes of the `CollectionPrinter<String>` activity:

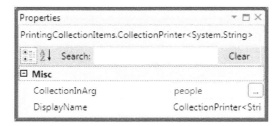

iv. Set the properties of the `ExistsInCollection<String>` activity:

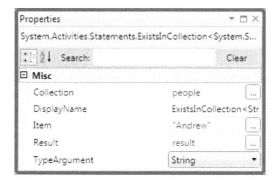

v. Set the `Text` property of the `WriteLine` activity as follows. By displaying the result value, we will know whether or not the item exists in the collection:

```
"Andrew exists in collection is " + result.ToString
```

3. Set `UsingExistsInCollectionActivity` as StartUp project and then press *Ctrl+F5* to run the project. We will see the following:

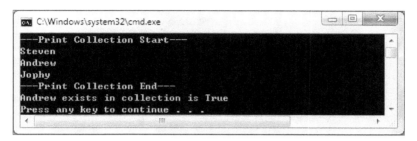

How it works...

It is a simple activity by which we can test whether or not a specified item exists in a particular collection object. Please note that we have to set the correct `TypeArgument` for this activity.

There's more

To use the `ExistsInCollection<T>` activity in code style workflow, open the `Program.cs` file and alter the code to:

```
using System;
using System.Activities;
using System.Activities.Statements;
using System.Collections.Generic;
using System.Activities.Expressions;
using PrintingCollectionItems;
namespace UsingExistsInCollectionActivity {
    class Program {
        static void Main(string[] args) {
            //WorkflowInvoker.Invoke(new Workflow1());
            WorkflowInvoker.Invoke(GetWFInstance());
        }
        static Activity GetWFInstance() {
            Variable<ICollection<String>> people = new
Variable<ICollection<string>>() {
                Default = new LambdaValue<ICollection<String>>(
                    ctx => new List<String> { "Steven", "Andrew",
                                               "Jophy" }
```

```
                        ),
                },
            Variable<Boolean> result = new Variable<Boolean>();
            Activity workflow = new Sequence() {
                Variables = { people, result },
                Activities = {
                    new CollectionPrinter<String>{
                        CollectionInArg=people
                    },
                    new ExistsInCollection<String>(){
                        Collection=people,
                        Item="Andrew",
                        Result=result
                    },
                    new WriteLine{
                        Text=new InArgument<string>(
                            aec=>"Andrew exists in collection is
"+result.Get(aec).ToString()
                        )
                    }
                }
            };
            return workflow;
        }
    }
}
```

Uncomment the following to run XAML-style workflow:

```
//WorkflowInvoker.Invoke(new Workflow1());
```

5
Custom Activities

This Chapter will cover:

- ▶ Creating an activity by inheriting the root activity
- ▶ Creating a FileWriter activity
- ▶ Creating a SendEmail activity
- ▶ Creating an Input Message activity using Bookmark
- ▶ Creating an Asynchronous HTTP Get activity
- ▶ Creating a Composite activity
- ▶ Creating an Activity Designer for the SendEmail activity
- ▶ Creating an Activity Designer for the MySequence activity

Introduction

Activity is the essence of workflow; even the workflow itself is an Activity. WF4 provides some build-in activities that can be used directly in the workflow designer panel. But many times, we need to create our own activities—for example, an activity that can send e-mail to inform someone about finishing a task or any other important thing. To define our own activity, we should write a class that implements the root abstract Activity or one of its predefined subclasses.

The following is the activity modeling class hierarchy diagram:

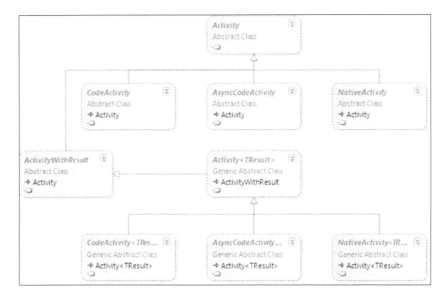

This chapter intends to provide readers not only with some additional activities besides the built-in activities, but also with some concepts on how to build our own activities.

Before moving ahead, please create two projects. The first is the ActivityLibrary project named `ActivityLibrary`.

The other is the Workflow Console Application named `WorkflowConsoleApp`.

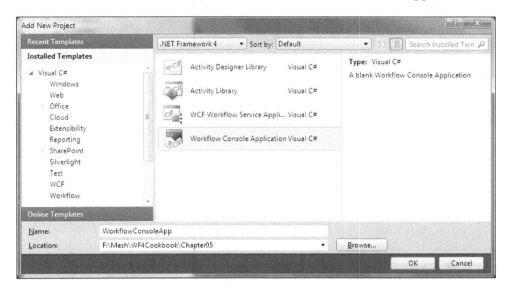

Delete `Workflow1.xaml`, which is created by default. We will use these two projects throughout this chapter. The `ActivityLibrary` project is for all customized activities, whereas the `WorkflowConsoleApp` project is used for testing our customized activities. The following screenshot shows the project structure:

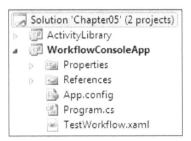

Creating an activity by inheriting the root activity

The abstract `Activity` class is the root of all subactivity classes. In this task, we will create a custom activity inheriting directly from `Activity`.

How to do it...

1. **Customize an Activity**:

    Add a new code file `MyActivity.cs` in the `ActivityLibrary` project, and fill the file with the following code:

    ```
    using System;
    using System.Activities;
    using System.Activities.Statements;
    public class MyActivity:Activity {
        public MyActivity() {
            this.Implementation = () => new Sequence {
                Activities = {
                    new WriteLine(){Text="Hello MyActivity"}
                }
            };
        }
    }
    ```

    Then build the activity project so that `MyActivity` appears in the toolbox panel of the workflow designer.

2. **Add a reference to ActivityLibrary**:

    In the `WorkflowConsoleApp` project, add an assembly reference to `ActivityLibrary` for us to be able to use these customized activities in the `WorkflowConsoleApp` project.

3. **Create a workflow to test the Activity**:

    Add a new workflow to `WorkflowConsoleApp` project and name it `TestMyActivityWF.xaml`. Please note that when we add a new workflow to the project, we actually select **Activity** in the **Add New Item** dialog.

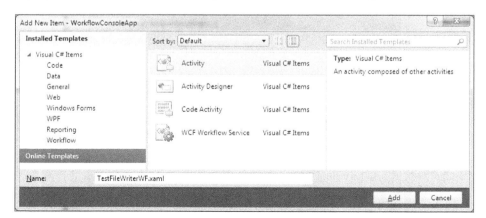

Now we can perform the following actions to create the workflow:

    i.   Drag a Sequence activity to the designer panel.

    ii.   Drag a `WriteLine` activity into the Sequence activity and input **Workflow start...** in the textbox.

    iii. Drag `MyActivity` below the `WriteLine` activity.

    iv. Drag a `WriteLine` activity below `MyActivity` and input **Workflow end...** in the textbox.

4. **Run it**:

Set `WorkflowConsoleApp` project as Startup project. Check the `Program.cs` file; the code should be like this:

```
class Program {
    static void Main(string[] args) {
        WorkflowInvoker.Invoke(new TestMyActivityWF());
    }
}
```

Press *Ctrl+F5* to run it. We should see the following:

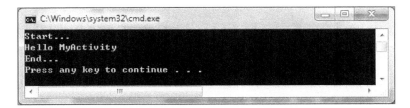

How it works...

The abstract `Activity` class is a base class for all activities in WF4. This abstract class defines the basic properties, method, and structure for all activities. We can directly create a concrete activity by inheriting this `Activity` class.

In real workflow applications, when we need a complex flow control activity that was not provided in the built-in activities, we can use this `Activity` class to create a new one.

There's more

We can also use the activity in code-style workflow:

```
class Program {
    static void Main(string[] args) {
        WorkflowInvoker.Invoke(GetCodeStyleWorkflow());
    }
    static Activity GetCodeStyleWorkflow() {
        Activity workflow = new Sequence {
            Activities ={
                new WriteLine{Text="Workflow start..."},
                new MyActivity(),
                new WriteLine{Text="Workflow end..."}
            }
        };
        return workflow;
    }
}
```

Creating a FileWriter activity

`CodeActivity` is an abstract class inherited from `Activity`. We can put our logic code in its `Execute` method. In this task, we are going to create an activity that will write data to a text file.

How to do it...

1. **Create the FileWriter activity**:

   Add a new code file to `ActivityLibrary` project named `FileWriter.cs`. Then replace all default code with the following code:

```
using System;
using System.Activities;
using System.Threading;
public sealed class FileWriter : CodeActivity {
    [RequiredArgument]
    public InArgument<string> fileName { get; set; }
    [RequiredArgument]
    public InArgument<string> fileData { get; set; }
    protected override void Execute(CodeActivityContext context) {
        string lines = fileData.Get(context);
        // Write the string to a file.
        System.IO.StreamWriter file =
            new System.IO.StreamWriter(fileName.Get(context));
        file.WriteLine(lines);
        //simulate writing process.
        Thread.Sleep(5000);
        file.Close();
    }
}
```

   We need to build the Activity project before using it in workflow.

2. **Create a workflow to test the FileWriter activity**:

   Add a new workflow to `WorkflowConsoleApp` project and name it
   `TestFileWriterWF.xaml`. Next, create a workflow as shown in the following
   screenshot:

   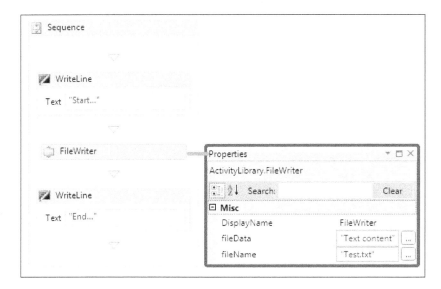

   Save and build the solution.

3. **Run it**:

   Alter the `Main` method of the `Program.cs` file as follows:

   ```
   static void Main(string[] args) {
       WorkflowInvoker.Invoke(new TestFileWriterWF());
   }
   ```

   Set `WorkflowConsoleApp` as Startup project. Next, press *Ctrl+F5* to run the
   workflow without debugging.

   Now, Navigate to the (...) `\WorkflowConsoleApp\bin\Debug`; we shall find a
   `Test.txt` file in this folder.

How it works...

Using `CodeActivity` is very simple; it is used to create simple leaf activities. The only thing we need to take care of is overriding the `Execute` method. The method will be called when the activity is executed.

There's more

We can also use the activity in code-style workflow:

```
class Program {
    static void Main(string[] args) {
        //WorkflowInvoker.Invoke(new TestFileWriterWF());
        WorkflowInvoker.Invoke(CodeStyleWorkflow());
    }
    static Activity CodeStyleWorkflow() {
        Activity workflow = new Sequence {
            Activities ={
                new WriteLine{Text="Start..."},
                new FileWriter{
                    fileName="Test.txt",
                    fileData="Text Content"
                },
                new WriteLine{Text="End..."}
            }
        };
        return workflow;
    }
}
```

Creating a SendEmail activity

In this task we are going to create an activity that can send an e-mail message to a target user.

How to do it...

1. **Create the SendEmail activity**:

   Add a new code file to the `ActivityLibrary` project named `SendEmail.cs`. Then, replace all code that is created by default with the following code:

   ```
   using System.Activities;
   public sealed class SendEmailActivity : CodeActivity {
       public InArgument<string> from { get; set; }
   ```

```
public InArgument<string> host { get; set; }
public InArgument<string> userName { get; set; }
public InArgument<string> password { get; set; }
public InArgument<string> to { get; set; }
public InArgument<string> subject { get; set; }
public InArgument<string> body { get; set; }
public OutArgument<string> result { get; set; }
protected override void Execute(CodeActivityContext context) {
    var mailMessage = new System.Net.Mail.MailMessage();
    mailMessage.To.Add(to.Get(context).ToString());
    mailMessage.Subject = subject.Get(context).ToString();
    mailMessage.Body = body.Get(context);
    mailMessage.From =
        new System.Net.Mail.MailAddress(from.Get(context));
    var smtp = new System.Net.Mail.SmtpClient();
    smtp.Host = host.Get(context);
    smtp.Credentials =
        new System.Net.NetworkCredential(
            userName.Get(context), password.Get(context));
    smtp.EnableSsl = true;
    smtp.Send(mailMessage);
    result.Set(context, "Sent Email Successfully!");
}
}
```

We need to build the activity project before using it in workflow.

2. **Create a workflow to test the SendEmail activity**:

Add a new workflow in the WorkflowConsoleApp project and name it
`TestSendEmailWF.xaml`. Create the workflow as shown in the following
screenshot:

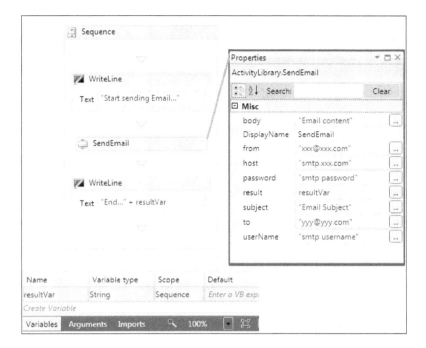

Save and build the solution.

3. **Run it:**

Alter the `Main` method of the `Program.cs` file to this:

```
static void Main(string[] args) {
    WorkflowInvoker.Invoke(new TestSendEmailWF());
}
```

Set `WorkflowConsoleApp` as Startup project. Next, press *Ctrl+F5* to run the workflow without debugging.

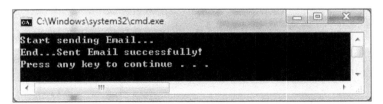

How it works...

Sending an e-mail usually costs some time. In real workflow applications, we should create an asynchronous activity or an independent WF service to send e-mail.

Creating an Input Message activity using Bookmark

When a workflow is running and we want to send a message to the workflow during run time, how can we achieve this? We can use Bookmark to achieve this. In this task, we will create an activity using Bookmark, which will function as a message input activity.

How to do it...

1. **Create the InputMessage activity**:

   Add a new code file to the `ActivityLibrary` project named `InputMessage.cs`. Then, replace all the default code with the following code:

```
using System.Activities;
public class InputMessage<T>:NativeActivity {
    public InArgument<string> bookmarkName { get; set; }
    public OutArgument<T> result { get; set; }
    protected override void Execute(NativeActivityContext context)
    {
        context.CreateBookmark(bookmarkName.Get(context),
                        new BookmarkCallback(
                        OnResumeBookmark));
    }
    public void OnResumeBookmark(NativeActivityContext context,
                        Bookmark bookmark,
                        object obj) {
        result.Set(context, (T)obj);
    }
    protected override bool CanInduceIdle {
        get { return true; }
    }
}
```

   Next, build the activity project so that `InputMessage` activity appears in the toolbox panel of the workflow designer.

2. **Create a workflow to test** `InputMessage` **activity**:

   Add a new workflow to the `WorkflowConsoleApp` project and name it `TestInputMessageWF.xaml`. Create a workflow as shown in the following screenshot:

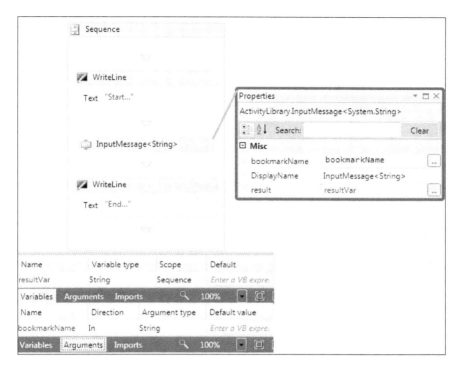

When we drag the `InputMessage<T>` activity to the workflow designer panel, we will see a dialog that will let us choose the type of the message we want to send to the workflow. In this task we choose **String**.

3. **Run it**:

Alter the `Main` method of the `Program.cs` file to this:

```
static void Main(string[] args) {
    AutoResetEvent waitHandler = new AutoResetEvent(false);
    string bkName = "inputBookmark";
    WorkflowApplication wfApp =
        new WorkflowApplication(new TestWorkflow() {
```

```
                    bookmarkName=bkName
        });
    wfApp.Completed = (arg) => { waitHandler.Set(); };
    wfApp.Run();
    wfApp.ResumeBookmark(bkName, Console.ReadLine());
    waitHandler.WaitOne();
}
```

Set `WorkflowConsoleApp` as Startup project. Next, press *Ctrl+F5* to run the workflow without debugging.

When the workflow runs, input **Hello bookmark** and the workflow prints the input message out.

How it works...

If we want to create an activity with Bookmark or a composite activity (for example, we want to create our own Sequence activity), then we should use `NativeActivity`. `NativeActivity` is more powerful and flexible than `CodeActivity`. However, we need to learn more about WF runtime and the `NativeActivity` class.

A bookmark is actually a named and resumable pause point. When an activity with a bookmark is executed, the activity will stop and wait for input. In workflow host, when the `ResumeBookmark` method (with parameters `bookmarkname` and input value) is called, the workflow will come out of the pause state and resume execution, and will keep executing until it competes or takes a pause for another bookmark.

Creating an Asynchronous HTTP Get activity

The `WebRequest` class enables us to make an HTTP request in code. Usually, every `WebRequest` call requires some time span—several seconds or even minutes. If there is only one request, we can wait for the response. But what are we going to do if we have to make more requests, say 100—every request uses several seconds, and so 100 requests will hang our program.

Then we come up with a good idea: why not use multiple threads with one request for each thread? But it is quite expensive to initialize a thread. If one is writing.NET-managed code, each thread will take up 1MB memory and so 100 threads will use up 100MB memory! Apparently, multiple threads are not an option. So what should we do? In this task, we will create a `CodeActivity` that can call a method asynchronously. The key is that our activity must inherit from `AsyncCodeActivity` (or `AsyncCodeActivity<T>`).

How to do it...

1. **Create the AsyncHttpGet activity**:

   Add a new code file named `AsyncHttpGet.cs` to the `ActivityLibrary` project. Then replace all default created code with the following code:

```
using System;
using System.Activities;
using System.Net;
using System.IO;
public class AsyncHttpGet: AsyncCodeActivity<string> {
    public InArgument<string> Uri { get; set; }
    protected override IAsyncResult BeginExecute(AsyncCodeActivity
Context context, AsyncCallback callback, object state) {
        WebRequest request = HttpWebRequest.Create(this.Uri.
                                                Get(context));
        context.UserState = request;
        return request.BeginGetResponse(callback, state);
    }

    protected override string EndExecute(AsyncCodeActivityContext
                                context, IAsyncResult result) {
        WebRequest request = context.UserState as WebRequest;
        using (WebResponse response = request.
            EndGetResponse(result))
        {
            using (StreamReader reader =
                new StreamReader(response.GetResponseStream())) {
                return reader.ReadToEnd();
            }
        }
    }
}
```

   Build the activity project before using it in workflow.

2. **Create a workflow to test the AsyncHttpGet activity**:

   Add a new workflow to the `WorkflowConsoleApp` project and name it
   `TestAsyncHttpGetWF.xaml`. Create a workflow as shown in the
   following screenshot:

3. **Run it:**

   Alter the `Main` method of the `Program.cs` file to this:

   ```
   static void Main(string[] args) {
       WorkflowInvoker.Invoke(new TestAsyncHttpGetWF());
   }
   ```

   Set `WorkflowConsoleApp` as Startup project. Next, press *Ctrl+F5* to run the
   workflow without debugging.

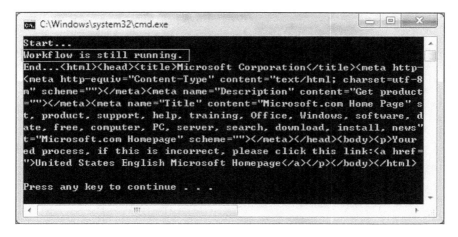

The message **Workflow is still running.** is a proof that the workflow is not blocked by the HTTP request.

How it works...

The `Sequence` activity will first call the `BeginExecute` method of `AsyncHttpGetActivity`, and pass a `callback` delegate. When the `BeginExecute` method finishes, it will return the `callback` delegate to its caller: `Sequence`. At the same time both the workflow and the HTTP request are executing asynchronously. Once the HTTP response data is ready, the `callback` delegate will be executed automatically. Now, the workflow knows that it is time to call the `EndExecute` method of `AsyncHttpGetActivity`.

Creating a Composite activity

There are many built-in composite activities in WF4 such as Sequence, While, Parallel, and so on. Is it possible to create our own composite activity? Well, the answer is we can. For demonstration purposes, we will create a `MySequence` activity in this task.

How to do it...

1. **Create the MySquence activity**:

   Add a new code file to the `ActivityLibrary` project named `MySequence.cs`. Then, replace all the default code with the following code:

   ```
   using System.Activities;
   using System.Collections.ObjectModel;
   namespace ActivityLibrary {
       public class MySequence:NativeActivity {
   ```

```
public Collection<Activity> Activities { get; set; }
public MySequence() {
    Activities = new Collection<Activity>();
}
int activityCounter = 0;
protected override void CacheMetadata(
                    NativeActivityMetadata metadata) {
    foreach (var activity in Activities) {
        metadata.AddImplementationChild(activity);
    }
}

protected override void Execute(NativeActivityContext
                                context)
{
    ScheduleActivities(context);
}

void ScheduleActivities(NativeActivityContext context) {
    if (activityCounter < Activities.Count)
        context.ScheduleActivity(this.
        Activities[activityCounter++],
        OnActivityCompleted);
}

void OnActivityCompleted(NativeActivityContext context,
                            ActivityInstance
completedInstance) {
        ScheduleActivities(context);
    }
  }
}
```

Build the activity project before using it in workflow.

2. **Create a code workflow to test the MySequence activity**:

Open the `Program.cs` file of the `WorkflowConsoleApp` project. Add a new method, `GetTestMySequenceWF`, to the Program class:

```
static Activity GetTestMySquenceWF() {
    return new MySequence() {
        Activities ={
            new WriteLine(){Text="WriteLine1"},
            new WriteLine(){Text="WriteLine2"},
            new WriteLine(){Text="WriteLine3"}
        }
```

```
        };
    }
```

3. **Run It**:

    Alter the `Main` method of the `Program.cs` file to this:

    ```
    static void Main(string[] args) {
        WorkflowInvoker.Invoke(GetTestMySquenceWF());
    }
    ```

    Set `WorkflowConsoleApp` as Startup project. Next, press *Ctrl+F5* to run the
    workflow without debugging.

How it works...

First and the most important thing to create a custom composite activity is that we should
inherit from `NativeActivity` (or `Activity`). We cannot create a composite activity using
`CodeActivity`.

The `metadata` object is used for storing workflow information. By accessing `metadata`, the
workflow instance is aware of its child activities, variables, and arguments. We can override
the `CacheMetaData` method so that we can register its child activities to the `metadata`:

```
foreach (var activity in Activities) {
    metadata.AddImplementationChild(activity);
}
```

In the `Execute` method, we will call the `ScheduleActivities` method. With the help of
`ScheduleActivities`, we can determine child activities' execution behavior.

We might get confused by the `OnActivitCompleted` method—why do we need such a
method, can we just schedule activities with the help of the following code ?

```
void ScheduleActivities(NativeActivityContext context) {
    for (int i = 0; i < Activities.Count; i++) {
        context.ScheduleActivity(this.Activities[i]);
    }
}
```

Well the answer is yes, we can schedule activities' in this way, but the child activities execution order will change to:

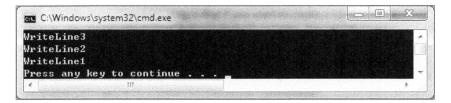

This is because the workflow runtime stores activities in a **stack** and the first scheduled activity will be executed last.

Creating an Activity Designer for the SendEmail activity

An Activity Designer is actually a surface of an activity in the workflow designer. We have already created a `SendEmail` to send an e-mail. In this task, we are going to create a designer (activity surface) for it. The final appearance will be like this:

Now, let's create it from scratch.

How to do it...

1. **Create an Activity Designer**:

   As Activity Designer is built upon WPF, we need to add references to `PresentationCore`, `PresentationFramework`, and `WindowsBase`. Add an **Activity Designer** item to the `ActivityLibrary` project and name it `SendEmailActivityDesigner.xaml`.

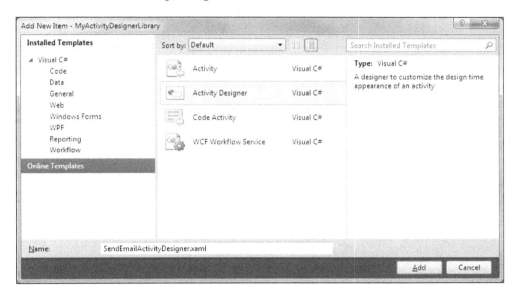

Now, open the code sample for this book and just copy the following code to replace the default created code in `SendEmailActivityDesigner.xaml`:

```
<sap:ActivityDesigner x:Class="ActivityLibrary.
SendEmailActivityDesigner"
    xmlns="http://schemas.microsoft.com/winfx/2006/xaml/
presentation"
    xmlns:x="http://schemas.microsoft.com/winfx/2006/xaml"
    xmlns:sap="clr-namespace:System.Activities.
Presentation;assembly=System.Activities.Presentation"
    xmlns:sapv="clr-namespace:System.Activities.Presentation.
View;assembly=System.Activities.Presentation"
    xmlns:sapc="clr-namespace:System.Activities.Presentation.
Converters;assembly=System.Activities.Presentation"
    xmlns:s="clr-namespace:System;assembly=mscorlib">
    <sap:ActivityDesigner.Resources>
        <sapc:ArgumentToExpressionConverter x:Key="ArgumentToExpre
ssionConverter"/>
```

```
            <DataTemplate x:Key="Collapsed">
                <StackPanel>
                    <TextBlock>This is the collapsed view</TextBlock>
                </StackPanel>
            </DataTemplate>
            <DataTemplate x:Key="Expanded">
                <StackPanel>
                    <Label Content="To"></Label>
                    <sapv:ExpressionTextBox
                        HintText="To:"
                        OwnerActivity="{Binding Path=ModelItem}"
                        Expression="{Binding Path=ModelItem.to,
                                        Mode=TwoWay,

Converter={StaticResource ArgumentToExpressionConverter },
                                        ConverterParameter=In}"

ExpressionType="s:String"/>
                    <Label Content="Subject:"></Label>
                    <sapv:ExpressionTextBox
                        HintText="Subject"
                        OwnerActivity="{Binding Path=ModelItem}"
                        Expression="{Binding Path=ModelItem.subject,
                                        Mode=TwoWay,

Converter={StaticResource ArgumentToExpressionConverter },
                                        ConverterParameter=In}"

ExpressionType="s:String"/>
                    <Label Content="Body:"></Label>
                    <sapv:ExpressionTextBox
                        HintText="Body"
                        OwnerActivity="{Binding Path=ModelItem}"
                        Expression="{Binding Path=ModelItem.body,
                                        Mode=TwoWay,

Converter={StaticResource ArgumentToExpressionConverter },
                                        ConverterParameter=In}"

ExpressionType="s:String" Height="100" />
                </StackPanel>
            </DataTemplate>
```

```
        <Style x:Key="ExpandOrCollapsedStyle"
                TargetType="{x:Type ContentPresenter}">
            <Setter Property="ContentTemplate"
                    Value="{DynamicResource Collapsed}"/>
            <Style.Triggers>
                <DataTrigger Binding="{Binding Path=ShowExpanded}"
Value="true">
                    <Setter Property="ContentTemplate"
Value="{DynamicResource Expanded}"/>
                </DataTrigger>
            </Style.Triggers>
        </Style>
    </sap:ActivityDesigner.Resources>
    <Grid>
        <ContentPresenter Style="{DynamicResource
ExpandOrCollapsedStyle}" Content="{Binding}" />
    </Grid>
</sap:ActivityDesigner>
```

Save and build the solution.

2. **Add a Designer attribute to the SendMail activity**:

   To connect this Activity Designer with the `SendMail` activity, we need to add a `Designer` attribute to the `SendEmail` activity.

```
using System.Activities;
using System.ComponentModel;
namespace ActivityLibrary {
    [Designer(typeof(SendEmailActivityDesigner))]
    public sealed class SendEmail : CodeActivity {
        public InArgument<string> from { get; set; }
        public InArgument<string> host { get; set; }
        public InArgument<string> userName { get; set; }
        public InArgument<string> password { get; set; }
        public InArgument<string> to { get; set; }
        public InArgument<string> subject { get; set; }
        public InArgument<string> body { get; set; }
        public OutArgument<string> result { get; set; }
        protected override void Execute(CodeActivityContext
                                    context) {
            var mailMessage = new System.Net.Mail.MailMessage();
            mailMessage.To.Add(to.Get(context).ToString());
            mailMessage.Subject = subject.Get(context).ToString();
            mailMessage.Body = body.Get(context);
            mailMessage.From =
                new System.Net.Mail.MailAddress(from.
                                        Get(context));
            var smtp = new System.Net.Mail.SmtpClient();
            smtp.Host = host.Get(context);
            smtp.Credentials =
```

```
                    new System.Net.NetworkCredential(userName.
                              Get(context), password.Get(context));
          smtp.EnableSsl = true;
          smtp.Send(mailMessage);
          result.Set(context, "Sent Email successfully!");
       }
     }
   }
```

Save and press *F6* to build the solution.

3. **Run it**:

   Now, open the `TestSendMailWF.xaml` file we created in a previous task. Fill out the e-mail properties. The final workflow appears as shown in the following screenshot:

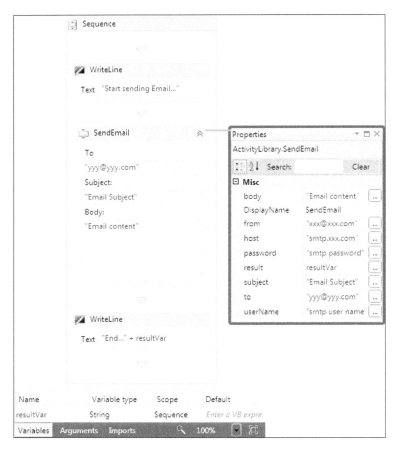

How it works...

This task demonstrates the following:

▶ Creating a custom Activity Designer with `ExpressionTextBox`:

```
<sapv:ExpressionTextBox
                    HintText="To:"
                    OwnerActivity="{Binding Path=ModelItem}"
                    Expression="{Binding Path=ModelItem.to,
                                    Mode=TwoWay,

    Converter={StaticResource ArgumentToExpressionConverter },
                                    ConverterParameter=In}"

    ExpressionType="s:String"/>
```

`ModelItem` is an object that can be used to draw workflow items in Workflow Designer. The following illustration describes the layer infrastructure of Workflow Designer (not Activity Designer):

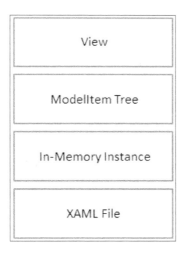

▶ Creating a custom Activity Designer with a "collapsed" and "expanded" view.

You can create a Activity Designer with a "collapsed" and "expanded" view by following the following XAML style:

```
<sap:ActivityDesigner x:Class="ActivityLibrary.ActivityDesigner1"
    ...>
    <sap:ActivityDesigner.Resources>
        <DataTemplate x:Key="Collapsed">
```

```
            <TextBlock>collapsed</TextBlock>
        </DataTemplate>
        <DataTemplate x:Key="Expanded">
            <TextBlock>Expanded</TextBlock>
        </DataTemplate>
        <Style x:Key="ExpandOrCollapsedStyle"
              TargetType="{x:Type ContentPresenter}">
            <Setter Property="ContentTemplate"
                  Value="{DynamicResource Collapsed}"/>
            <Style.Triggers>
                <DataTrigger Binding="{Binding Path=ShowExpanded}"
Value="true">
                    <Setter Property="ContentTemplate"
Value="{DynamicResource Expanded}"/>
                </DataTrigger>
            </Style.Triggers>
        </Style>
    </sap:ActivityDesigner.Resources>
    <Grid>
        <ContentPresenter Style="{DynamicResource
ExpandOrCollapsedStyle}" Content="{Binding}" />
    </Grid>
</sap:ActivityDesigner>
```

Define all possible views and present style under `DataTemplate` element. Under `Grid` element, use a `ContentPrensenter` to represent the final view.

Creating an Activity Designer for the MySquence activity

We have already created a `MySequence` activity in a previous task. In this task, we are going to create a designer for it.

How to do it...

1. **Create an Activity Designer**:

   Add an **Activity Designer** item to the `ActivityLibrary` project and name it `MySequenceDesigner.xaml`. Use the following code to replace the default generated code:

   ```
   <sap:ActivityDesigner x:Class="ActivityLibrary.MySequenceDesigner"
   ```

```
    xmlns="http://schemas.microsoft.com/winfx/2006/xaml/
presentation"
    xmlns:x="http://schemas.microsoft.com/winfx/2006/xaml"
    xmlns:sap="clr-namespace:System.Activities.
Presentation;assembly=System.Activities.Presentation"
    xmlns:sapv="clr-namespace:System.Activities.Presentation.
View;assembly=System.Activities.Presentation">
    <Grid>
        <StackPanel>
            <sap:WorkflowItemsPresenter HintText="Drop Activities
                                                   Here"
                                        Items="{Binding
Path=ModelItem.Activities,Mode=TwoWay}">
                <sap:WorkflowItemsPresenter.SpacerTemplate>
                    <DataTemplate>
                        <Ellipse Width="20" Height="20"
Fill="Black"/>
                    </DataTemplate>
                </sap:WorkflowItemsPresenter.SpacerTemplate>
                <sap:WorkflowItemsPresenter.ItemsPanel>
                    <ItemsPanelTemplate>
                        <StackPanel Orientation="Vertical"/>
                    </ItemsPanelTemplate>
                </sap:WorkflowItemsPresenter.ItemsPanel>
            </sap:WorkflowItemsPresenter>
        </StackPanel>
    </Grid>
</sap:ActivityDesigner>
```

2. **Add a Designer attribute for the MySequence activity**:

   To connect this Activity Designer with the MySequence activity, we need to add a Designer attribute for the MySequence activity. Add the following statement right above the MySequence class definition:

   ```
   [Designer(typeof(MySequenceDesigner))]
   ```

   Save the solution and build it by pressing the *F6* key.

3. **Create a workflow to test the MySequence activity**:

Add a new workflow to the `WorkflowConsoleApp` project and name it `TestMySequenceWF.xaml`. Create the workflow as shown in the following screenshot:

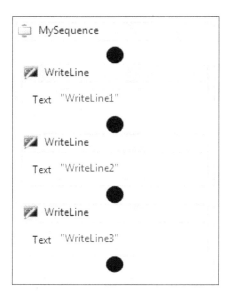

Save and build the project.

4. **Run it**:

Alter the `Main` method of the `Program.cs` file to this:

```
static void Main(string[] args) {
    WorkflowInvoker.Invoke(new TestMySequenceWF());
}
```

Set `WorkflowConsoleApp` as Startup project. Next, press *Ctrl+F5* to run the workflow without debugging.

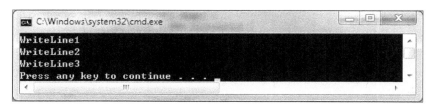

How it works...

This task demonstrates creating a custom activity using `WorkflowItemsPresenter`.

By using `WorkflowItemsPresenter`, we can create an activity that contains multiple activities.

We can define our spacer template in `SpacerTemplate`. In this task, we use a black circle to represent the spacer. If we wish to create a triangle spacer, we need to replace the following:

```
<Ellipse Width="20" Height="20" Fill="Black"/>
```

with the following:

```
<Path Margin="0,15,0,0"
      Stretch="Fill"
      StrokeMiterLimit="2.75"
      Stroke="#FFA8B3C2" Fill="#FFFFFFFF"
         Data="F1 M 675.738,744.979L 665.7,758.492L 655.66,744.979L
675.738,744.979 Z "
         Width="16" Height="10" />
```

Now save and build the project. The `TestMySequenceWF` workflow will appear like this:

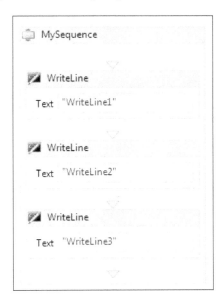

6
WF4 Extensions

This chapter will cover:

- ▸ Configuring ETW tracking
- ▸ Creating a FileTrackingParticipant
- ▸ Configuring the SQL persistence store
- ▸ Loading a persisted workflow from the database
- ▸ Using a persistence participant to persist additional data
- ▸ Using a customized extension

Introduction

The focus of this chapter is WF4 tracking and persistence. In the old WF3, we usually call them as services. In WF4, these features are implemented as extensions. The term "service" in WF4 usually refers to WCF service.

The Tracking extension in WF4 can record the "foot prints" of the execution of a workflow instance. The Persistence extension in WF4 can save running workflow instances in durable storage such as a database or disk file.

Configuring ETW tracking

ETW stands for **Event Tracing for Windows**. Simply put, ETW tracking means our ability to see tracking information in the famous Event Viewer.

Getting ready

We need Windows Vista, Windows 7, or Windows Server 2008 to perform this task.

How to do it...

1. **Create a Workflow Console Application project**:

   Create a new Workflow Console Application project and name it
   ConfiguringETWTracking. Name the solution as Chapter06.

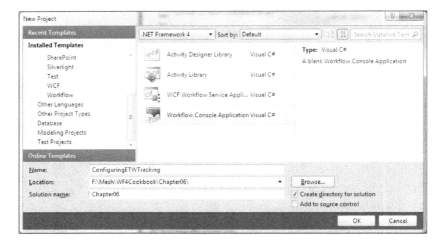

2. **Author a workflow**:

   Open the Workflow1.xaml file, which is created by default, and create an extremely
   simple workflow just for tracking.

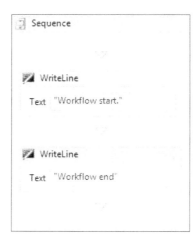

3. **Enable ETW tracking:**

    Open **Event Viewer**, navigate to **Event Viewer | Applications and Services Logs | Microsoft | Windows | Application Server-Applications**. Right-click **Application Server-Applications** and select **View | Show Analytic and Debug Logs**. After refreshing the node, we should see:

4. **Create a workflow host**:

    Open `Program.cs` file, and fill the file with the following code:

```
using System.Activities.Tracking;
using System.Threading;
using System.Activities;
namespace ConfiguringETWTracking {
    class Program {
        static void Main(string[] args) {
            #region ETW tracking setup
            TrackingProfile trackingProfile =
                                new TrackingProfile();
```

```
{
                         trackingProfile.Queries.Add(new WorkflowInstanceQuery

                             States = { "*" }
                         });
                         trackingProfile.Queries.Add(new ActivityStateQuery {
                             States = { "*" }
                         });
                         trackingProfile.Queries.Add(new CustomTrackingQuery {
                             ActivityName = "*",
                             Name = "*"
                         });
                         EtwTrackingParticipant etwTrackingParticipant =
                             new EtwTrackingParticipant();
                         etwTrackingParticipant.TrackingProfile =
                                                     trackingProfile;
                         #endregion

                         #region Workflow Application
                         AutoResetEvent waitHandler = new
                                                 AutoResetEvent(false);
                         WorkflowApplication wfApp =
                             new WorkflowApplication(new Workflow1());
                         wfApp.Completed = (arg) => { waitHandler.Set(); };
                         wfApp.Extensions.Add(etwTrackingParticipant);
                         wfApp.Run();
                         waitHandler.WaitOne();
                         #endregion
                     }
                 }
             }
```

5. **Run it**:

Press *Ctrl+F5* to run the workflow. After running the workflow, right-click the **Analytic** node, and select **Refresh**. We will see the following:

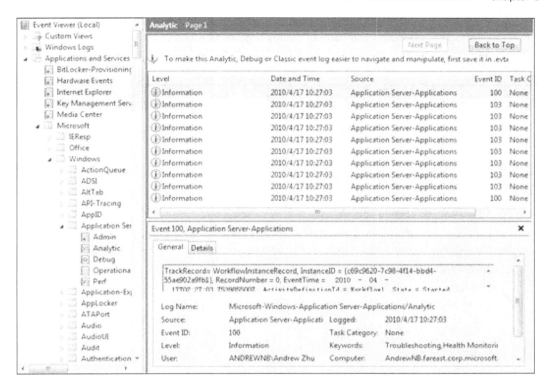

How it works...

To understand WF4 tracking, we need to understand three primary components:

- The `TrackingRecord` object holds all the tracking data.

- `TrackingParticipant` provides methods to access `TrackingRecord`. In this task, `EtwTrackingParticipant` is a specified `TrackingParticipant`, using which the workflow host can emit tracking records to the event viewer.

- `TrackingProfile` functions as a filter in the tracking process. In this task, we created a `TrackingProfile` that will tell `TrackingParticipant` to record workflow instance states, activity states, and custom tracking states, rather than using "*" to represent all workflow instance state items. We can use predefined keywords to record states we need. Consider the following example:

```
trackingProfile.Queries.Add(new WorkflowInstanceQuery {

    States = { "Started","Idel","Persisted","Resumed","Unloaded" }

});
```

To get the full list of workflow instance states, please check the MSDN document available at `http://msdn.microsoft.com/en-us/library/system.activities.tracking.workflowinstancequery.states(v=VS.100).aspx`.

Creating FileTrackingParticipant

We may want to create our own tracking participant and store tracking information in a text file. In this task, we are going to create such a tracking participant.

How to do it...

1. **Create a workflow project**:

   Create a new Workflow Console Application under the solution `Chapter06` and name the project `CreatingFileTrackingParticipant`.

2. **Author a workflow**:

   Open the `Workflow1.xaml` file, which is created by default, and create an extremely simple workflow just for tracking.

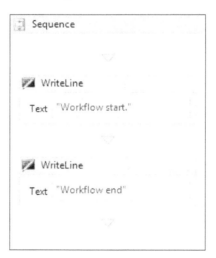

3. **Create a custom tracking participant—FileTrackingParticipant.cs**:

   Now, create a class file and name it `FileTrackingParticipant.cs` containing the following code

```
using System.Activities.Tracking;
using System;
using System.IO;
namespace FileTrackingParticipant {
```

```
public class FileTrackingParticipant:TrackingParticipant {
    string fileName;
    protected override void Track(TrackingRecord record,
                                  TimeSpan timeout) {
        fileName = @"c:\" + record.InstanceId + ".tracking";
        using (StreamWriter sw = File.AppendText(fileName)) {
            sw.WriteLine("----------Tracking
Started-----------");
            sw.WriteLine(record.ToString());
            sw.WriteLine("----------Tracking End--------------
-");
        }
    }
}
}
```

4. **Create a workflow host**:

   Open the `Program.cs` file and alter its code to:

```
class Program {
static void Main(string[] args) {
TrackingProfile fileTrackingProfile = new TrackingProfile();
fileTrackingProfile.Queries.Add(new WorkflowInstanceQuery {
States = { "*" }
});
fileTrackingProfile.Queries.Add(new ActivityStateQuery() {
States = {
ActivityStates.Executing,
ActivityStates.Closed
}
});
FileTrackingParticipantfileTrackingParticipant =
newFileTrackingParticipant();
fileTrackingParticipant.TrackingProfile = fileTrackingProfile;
AutoResetEventwaitHandler = new AutoResetEvent(false);
WorkflowApplicationwfapp =
new WorkflowApplication (new Workflow1());
wfapp.Unloaded = (wfAppEventArg) =>{ waitHandler.Set(); };
        wfapp.Extensions.Add(fileTrackingParticipant);
        wfapp.Run();
```

```
                    waitHandler.WaitOne();
          }
     }
```

5. **Run it**:

    Press *Ctrl+F5* to run the project without debugging. After running, we can see a file suffixed with `.tracking` in directory `c:\`.

How it works...

To create a custom tracking participant, the key is overriding the `Tracking` method. In this method, we can write code to store tracking information to any place of our choice. In the `Tracking` method, we can manipulate the tracking data in a lot of ways— for example e-mail it or send it out by web service.

Configuring the SQL persistence store

In real-world applications, to make sure the performance meets requirements, it is recommended to use a database as the workflow persistence store. WF4 has a built-in SQL persistence store type. All we need to do is some configurations.

Getting ready

SQL Server (include express edition) 2005/2008 is needed to perform this task.

How to do it...

1. **Create a workflow project**:

    Create a new Workflow Console Application under solution `Chapter06` and name the project as `ConfiguringSqlPersistenceStore`.

2. **Set up a persistence database**:

    We can find SQL scripts in `%WINDIR%\Microsoft.NET\Framework\v4.xxx\SQL\EN`. In this folder, only two files are needed: `SqlWorkflowInstanceStoreSchema.sql` and `SqlWorkflowInstanceStoreLogic.sql`.

    We first execute `SqlWorkflowInstanceStoreSchema.sql` and then execute `SqlWorkflowInstanceStoreLogic.sql`. We can execute these SQL files in Visual Studio or SQL Server Management Studio. I would prefer to write a batch file to do all these steps. We need to create a SQL file to create a SQL persistence database:

i. Create a file named `CreateSqlPersistenceDatabase.sql` in any folder containing the following SQL statements.

```
Use Master
Go
IF EXISTS (SELECT *
        FROM    master..sysdatabases
        WHERE   name = N'PersistenceDatabase')
    DROP DATABASE PersistenceDatabase
GO
CREATE DATABASE PersistenceDatabase
GO
```

ii. In the same folder, create a batch file named `SetupSqlPersistenceStore.bat` containing the following commands.

```
echo Create SQL persistence database...
sqlcmd -S %COMPUTERNAME%\SQLEXPRESS -E -n -i
"CreateSqlPersistenenceDatabase.sql"

echo Execute SqlWorkflowInstanceStoreSchema.sql
sqlcmd -S %COMPUTERNAME%\SQLEXPRESS -E -n -d
PersistenceDatabase -i "SqlWorkflowInstanceStoreSchema.sql"

echo Execute SqlWorkflowInstanceStoreLogic.sql
sqlcmd -S %COMPUTERNAME%\SQLEXPRESS -E -n -d
PersistenceDatabase -i "SqlWorkflowInstanceStoreLogic.sql"

::Pause
```

iii. Before running the batch file, we need to copy `SqlWorkflowInstanceStoreSchema.sql` and `SqlWorkflowInstanceStoreLogic.sql` to the same folder as that of the `SetupSqlPersistence.bat` file.

Double-click `SetupSqlPersistenceStore.bat` and the database will be set up.

3. **Create a workflow**:

Open the `Workflow1.xaml` file, which is created by default, and create a simple workflow with a delay activity.

Set the `Duration` property of the `Delay` activity to 1 second. Once the `Delay` activity is executed, the workflow will become idle and the whole workflow instance will be persisted in the database.

4. **Create a workflow host**:

Add project references to `System.Activities.DurableInstancing` and `System.Runtime.DurableInstancing`. Open the `Program.cs` file and alter the code to:

```
using System.Activities.DurableInstancing;
using System.Threading;
using System.Activities;
namespace ConfiguringSqlPersistenceStore {
    class Program {
        static void Main(string[] args) {
            //setup sql persistence store
            string sqlPersistenceDBConnectionString=
                @"Data Source=.\sqlexpress;
                    Initial Catalog=PersistenceDatabase;
                    Integrated Security=True";
            SqlWorkflowInstanceStore sqlWFInstanceStore =
```

```
            new SqlWorkflowInstanceStore(
                        sqlPersistenceDBConnectionString);
        //create and run workflow application
        AutoResetEvent waitHandler = new
                    AutoResetEvent(false);
        WorkflowApplication wfApp =
            new WorkflowApplication(new Workflow1());
        wfApp.InstanceStore = sqlWFInstanceStore;
        wfApp.Unloaded = (arg) => {
            waitHandler.Set();
        };
        wfApp.PersistableIdle = (arg) => {
            return PersistableIdleAction.Unload;
        };
        wfApp.Run();
        waitHandler.WaitOne();
    }
}
}
```

5. **Run it**:

    Press *Ctrl+F5* to run the project without debugging. The running workflow instance will be persisted in the database once the `Delay` activity is executed. We can query the `[System.Activities.DurableInstancing].InstancesTable` table against the `PersistenceDatabase` database to see the persisted workflow instance data.

How it works...

The `Delay` activity can induce the workflow to be idle, and the workflow will be persisted in the persistence store. Please note that after the workflow is persisted and unloaded from memory, the workflow instance will not be resumed from the persistence store even after the delay time. We need to resume the workflow instance manually or we can write a host service to monitor the time and perform the task of resuming the workflow.

Loading a persisted workflow from the database

Developing long-running applications is one goal of WF4, and resuming a persisted workflow from the database is the key to long-running applications. In this task, we will create a Sequence workflow with a Delay activity. The workflow will be persisted when it is idle. We then press the *Enter* key and then the workflow will be resumed and will run until its end.

Getting ready

The SQL workflow instance store needs to be already in use. We can refer the *Configuring the SQL persistence store* section of this chapter.

How to do it...

1. **Create a workflow project**:

   Create a new Workflow Console Application under solution `Chapter06` and name the project as `LoadingUpWorkflowFromPersistenceDB`.

2. **Create a workflow:**

   Open the `Workflow1.xaml` file, which is created by default, and create a simple workflow with a `Delay` activity.

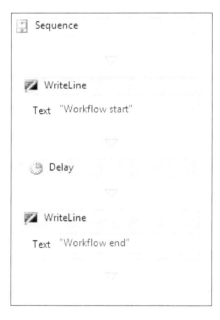

   Set the `Duration` property of `Delay` activity to 1 second. Once the Delay activity is executed, the workflow will become idle and the whole workflow instance will be persisted in the database.

3. **Create a workflow Host**:

   Add project references to `System.Activities.DurableInstancing` and `System.Runtime.DurableInstancing`. Open the `Program.cs` file and alter the code to:

```
class Program {
    static SqlWorkflowInstanceStore sqlWorkflowInstanceStore =
        SetupSqlPersistenceStore();
    static void Main(string[] args) {
        StartAndUnloadInstance();
    }
    static void StartAndUnloadInstance() {
        AutoResetEvent waitHandler = new AutoResetEvent(false);
        WorkflowApplication wfApp = new WorkflowApplication(new
                                Workflow1());
        wfApp.InstanceStore = sqlWorkflowInstanceStore;
        wfApp.PersistableIdle = (e) => {
            return PersistableIdleAction.Unload;
        };
        wfApp.Unloaded = (e) => {
            waitHandler.Set();
        };
        Guid id = wfApp.Id;
        wfApp.Run();
        waitHandler.WaitOne();
        LoadAndCompleteInstance(id);
    }
    static void LoadAndCompleteInstance(Guid id) {
        Console.WriteLine("Press <enter> to load the persisted
                        workflow");
        Console.ReadLine();
        AutoResetEvent waitHandler = new AutoResetEvent(false);
        WorkflowApplication wfApp = new WorkflowApplication(new
                                Workflow1());
        wfApp.InstanceStore = sqlWorkflowInstanceStore;
        wfApp.Unloaded = (workflowApplicationEventArgs) => {
            waitHandler.Set();
        };
        wfApp.Load(id);
        wfApp.Run();
        waitHandler.WaitOne();
    }
    private static SqlWorkflowInstanceStore
SetupSqlPersistenceStore() {
        string connectionString =
            @"Data Source=.\sqlexpress;
```

```
                    Initial Catalog=PersistenceDatabase;
                    Integrated Security=True";
            SqlWorkflowInstanceStore sqlWFInstanceStore =
                new SqlWorkflowInstanceStore(connectionString);
            sqlWFInstanceStore.InstanceCompletionAction =
                InstanceCompletionAction.DeleteAll;
            return sqlWFInstanceStore;
        }
    }
```

4. **Run it**:

    Before running it, we need to make sure that we have replaced the SQL connection string with our own one. Then, press *Ctrl+F5* to run the project without debugging.

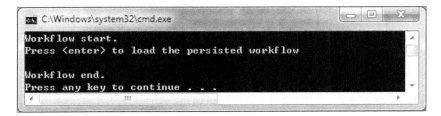

How it works...

In the `StartAndUnloadInstance` method, we may want to use the following statement to persist a workflow instance:

```
wfApp.PersistableIdle = (e) => {
    return PersistableIdleAction.Persist;
};
```

Instead of `return PersistableIdleAction.Unload;`, the persisted workflow will be locked by the instance owner, and the workflow will exit without unloading. The consequence is, if we try to load a locked workflow instance from the database with a new `WorkflowApplication` object, we will get the following exception:

Unhandled Exception: System.Runtime.DurableInstancing.InstanceLockedException: The execution of an InstancePersistenceCommand was interrupted because the instance 'xxxxxxxx-xxxx-xxxx-xxxx-xxxxxxxxx' is locked by a different instance owner. This error usually occurs because a different host has the instance loaded. The instance owner ID of the owner or host with a lock on the instance is 'xxxxxxxx-xxxx-xxxx-xxxx-xxxxxxxxxxxx'.

If we want to persist a workflow and unload the workflow from the memory, we should use `PersistableIdelAction.Unload` instead of `PersistableIdleAction.Persist`.

If we are going to have multiple hosts potentially loading the same workflow instance, we need to specify the instance store's `DefaultInstanceOwner`:

```
InstanceHandle handle = instanceStore.CreateInstanceHandle();
InstanceView view=instanceStore.Execute(handle,new CreateWorkflowOwner
Command(),TimeSpan.FromSeconds(5));
handle.Free();
instanceStore.DefaultInstanceOwner=view.InstanceOwner
```

There's more

This is the execution sequence of persistence-related events:

- ▶ PersisteableIdle
- ▶ Idle
- ▶ Completed (optional)
- ▶ Unloaded (optional)

Using a persistence participant to persist additional data

When the workflow instance is persisted, some additional data may need to be persisted along with the workflow instance. For example, in web applications, different HTTP requests are initialized by different people. So, to make sure our workflow instance is aware of its owner, we should store the user information along with the workflow instance.

Getting ready

We need to make sure we have finished the task of *Loading a persisted workflow from the database*, which we have seen earlier in this chapter.

How to do it...

1. **Create a workflow project**:

   Create a new Workflow Console Application under solution `Chapter06` and name the project as `UsingPersistenceParticipant`.

2. **Create a custom persistence participant**:

Add project references to `System.Activities.DurableInstancing` and `System.Runtime.DurableInstancing`. Add a new code file to project and name the file `MyPersistenceParticipant.cs`. Fill the file with the following code:

```
usingSystem.Activities.Persistence;
usingSystem.Xml.Linq;
usingSystem.Collections.Generic;
using System;
namespaceUsingPersistenceParticipant {
public class MyPersistenceParticipant : PersistenceParticipant {
public string message;
staticXNamespacedataNamespace =
XNamespace.Get("http://xhinker.com/");
protected override void CollectValues(out IDictionary<XName,
object>readWriteValues,
outIDictionary<XName, object>writeOnlyValues) {
readWriteValues = new Dictionary<XName, object>();
readWriteValues.Add(dataNamespace. GetName("messageXName"), this.
message);
writeOnlyValues = null;
}
protected override IDictionary<XName, object>MapValues(
IDictionary<XName, object>readWriteValues,
IDictionary<XName, object>writeOnlyValues) {
returnbase.MapValues(readWriteValues, writeOnlyValues);
}
protected override void PublishValues(
IDictionary<XName, object>readWriteValues) {
Console.WriteLine("message:" +
readWriteValues[dataNamespace. GetName("messageXName")]);
}
}
}
```

3. **Create a custom CodeActivity**:

Add a new code file containing the following code to the project and name it `CollectDataActivity.cs`. This activity is used for collecting data when workflow runs.

```
using System.Activities;
namespace UsingPersistenceParticipant
{
    public sealed class CollectDataActivity : CodeActivity
    {
        protected override void Execute
                        (CodeActivityContext context)
        {
            context.GetExtension
                <MyPersistenceParticipant>().message =
                "hello persistence participant";
        }
    }
}
```

Build the project so that we can use `CollectDataActivity` in workflow.

4. **Create a workflow—Workflow1.xaml:**

   Open `Workflow1.xaml`, which is created by default, and author a workflow as shown in the following screenshot:

5. **Create a workflow host**:

Open the `Program.cs` file and alter the code to:

```
using System.Activities.DurableInstancing;
using System.Xml.Linq;
using System.Threading;
using System.Activities;
using System;
using System.Collections.Generic;
using System.Runtime.DurableInstancing;
namespace UsingPersistenceParticipant {
    class Program {
        static SqlWorkflowInstanceStore sqlWorkflowInstanceStore =
            SetupSqlpersistenceStore();
        static XNamespace dataNamespace = null;
        static void Main(string[] args) {
            StartAndUnloadInstance();
        }
        static void StartAndUnloadInstance() {
            AutoResetEvent waitHandler = new
                        AutoResetEvent(false);
            WorkflowApplication wfApp = new
                        WorkflowApplication(new Workflow1());
            wfApp.InstanceStore = sqlWorkflowInstanceStore;
            wfApp.Extensions.Add(new MyPersistenceParticipant());
            wfApp.PersistableIdle = (e) => {
                return PersistableIdleAction.Unload;
            };
            wfApp.Unloaded = (e) => {
                waitHandler.Set();
            };
            Guid id = wfApp.Id;
            wfApp.Run();
            waitHandler.WaitOne();
            LoadAndCompleteInstance(id);
        }
        static void LoadAndCompleteInstance(Guid id) {
            Console.WriteLine("Press <enter> to load the persisted
                        workflow");
            Console.ReadLine();
            AutoResetEvent waitHandler = new
                        AutoResetEvent(false);
```

```
            WorkflowApplication wfApp = new
                        WorkflowApplication(new Workflow1());
            wfApp.InstanceStore = sqlWorkflowInstanceStore;
            wfApp.Extensions.Add(new MyPersistenceParticipant());
            wfApp.Unloaded = (workflowApplicationEventArgs) =>
            {
                waitHandler.Set();
            };
            wfApp.Load(id);
            wfApp.Run();
            waitHandler.WaitOne();
        }
        private static SqlWorkflowInstanceStore
                    SetupSqlpersistenceStore()
        {

            string connectionString =
                    @"Data Source=.\sqlexpress;
                Initial Catalog=PersistenceDatabase;
                Integrated Security=True";
            SqlWorkflowInstanceStore sqlWFInstanceStore =
                new SqlWorkflowInstanceStore(connectionString);
            dataNamespace = XNamespace.Get("http://xhinker.com/");

            List<XName> variantProperties = new List<XName>();
            variantProperties.Add(dataNamespace.
                            GetName("messageXName"));
            sqlWFInstanceStore.Promote("additionalProperty",
                            variantProperties, null);
            sqlWFInstanceStore.InstanceCompletionAction =
                InstanceCompletionAction.DeleteAll;

            InstanceHandle handle = sqlWFInstanceStore.
                            CreateInstanceHandle();
            InstanceView view = sqlWFInstanceStore.Execute(handle,
                new CreateWorkflowOwnerCommand(),

TimeSpan.FromSeconds(5));
            handle.Free();
            sqlWFInstanceStore.DefaultInstanceOwner =
                            view.InstanceOwner;
            return sqlWFInstanceStore;
        }
    }
}
```

6. **Run it**:

Set `UsingPersistenceParticipant` as the Startup project and press *Ctrl+F5* to run the project. We will see the following before pressing the *Enter* key:

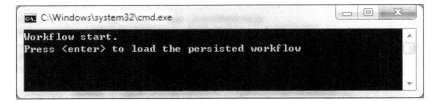

Now open the `InstancePromotedPropertiesTable` table of the persistence database. We will see a data row that stores the collected data: **hello persistence participant**. Once back to the application console and after pressing the *Enter* key, we will see the following:

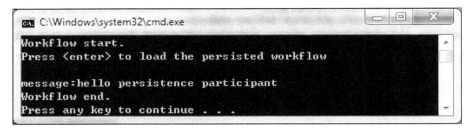

How it works...

A persistence participant will be triggered by the workflow application host when the workflow instance is saved into or loaded from durable storage.

We need to understand three key methods in the `MyPersistenceParticipant` class.

- `CollectValues`: This method will be called first. We can use this method to collect data that needs to be persisted along with the workflow instance.

- `MapValues`: This method will be called following the `CollectValues` method. Usually, we need to use only the following:

  ```
  return base.MapValues(readWriteValues, writeOnlyValues);
  ```

  Now all the collected data will automatically be stored in the persistence store. We can also store data in some other durable store by writing I/O code.

- `PublishValues`: This method will be called when the workflow is resumed from the persistence store.

Using a customized extension

WF4 also allows us to define our own WF4 extensions. In this task, we will create a simple extension and use this extension in a workflow.

How to do it...

1. **Create a Workflow Console Application**:

   Add a new Workflow Console Application to the `Chapter06` solution and name it `UsingCustomizedExtension`.

2. **Create a customized extension**:

   Add a new code file to the project and name the file `SimpleExtension.cs`. Fill the file with the following code:

```
using System.Activities.Hosting;
using System.Collections.Generic;
using System;
namespace UsingCustomizedExtension {
    public class SimpleExtension : IWorkflowInstanceExtension {
        private WorkflowInstanceProxy instance;
        public IEnumerable<object> GetAdditionalExtensions() {
            return null;
        }
        public void SetInstance(WorkflowInstanceProxy instance) {
            this.instance = instance;
        }
        public void DoSomething() {
            Console.WriteLine("Extension is doing something...");
        }
    }
}
```

3. **Create a custom activity that will use the customized extension**:

   Add a new code file to the project and name it `UseSimpleExtension.cs`. Then fill the file with the following code:

```
using System.Activities;
using UsingCustomizedExtension;
public class UseSimpleExtension : NativeActivity {
    protected override void Execute(NativeActivityContext context)
    {
        var extension = context.GetExtension<SimpleExtension>();
```

```
                    extension.DoSomething();
            }
    }
```

Build the project so that the customized activity will appear in the toolbox.

4. **Author a Workflow:**

   Open the `Workflow1.xaml` file, which is created by default, and author a workflow as shown as the following screenshot:

5. **Create host code:**

   Open the `Program.cs` file and alter its code to:

```
using System.Threading;
using System.Activities;
namespace UsingCustomizedExtension {
    class Program {
        static void Main(string[] args) {
            AutoResetEvent waitHandler = new
                            AutoResetEvent(false);
            WorkflowApplication wfApp =
                new WorkflowApplication(new Workflow1());
            wfApp.Unloaded = (e) => {
                waitHandler.Set();
```

```
        };
        wfApp.Extensions.Add(new SimpleExtension());
        wfApp.Run();
        waitHandler.WaitOne();
      }
    }
  }
```

6. **Run it**:

   Set `UsingCustomizedExtension` as Startup project and press *Ctrl+F5* to run it without debugging. We should see the following:

How it works...

`SimpleExtension`, implementer of the `IWorkflowInstanceExtension`, will be called by the `WorkflowApplication` class (which is an implementer of the abstract class `WorkflowInstance`), before the workflow's execution. This makes sure extensions are registered to the workflow instance. The following code actually registers a workflow extension:

```
wfApp.Extensions.Add(new SimpleExtension());
```

As an extension instance is already registered in the workflow instance context, we can call the extension instance in a customized activity:

```
protected override void Execute(NativeActivityContext context) {
    var extension = context.GetExtension<SimpleExtension>();
    extension.DoSomething();
}
```

There's more

When we are creating workflow services (XAMLX files), we can drop those XAMLX files directly into the IIS virtual directory without host code. So, the question is, can we add our own extensions to workflow service? Well the answer is, YES, we can add our extensions in the CacheMetadata method of a customized activity. Consider the following as an example:

```
using System.Activities;
using UsingCustomizedExtension;
public class UseSimpleExtension : NativeActivity {
    protected override void CacheMetadata(NativeActivityMetadata
      metadata)
    {
        metadata.AddDefaultExtensionProvider<SimpleExtension>(
            ()=>new SimpleExtension()
        );
    }
    protected override void Execute(NativeActivityContext context) {
        var extension = context.GetExtension<SimpleExtension>();
        extension.DoSomething();
    }
}
```

7

Hosting Workflow Applications

In this chapter, we will cover:

- ▶ Hosting a workflow service in IIS7
- ▶ Hosting workflow in ASP.NET
- ▶ Hosting workflow in WPF
- ▶ Hosting workflow in a Windows Form

Introduction

WF4 is one part of .NET Framework 4.0, which means WF4 workflow can be hosted and run in any type of application running with the .NET framework. We can host a workflow as a WCF service. We can also invoke a workflow service from a workflow or host workflow in an ASP.NET application and handle all the business logic behind the page.

When we design workflow applications, please let workflow be workflow. Don't couple workflow with other logic. For example, in this chapter, hosting workflow in ASP.NET is for conception demonstration only, not the best practice. In the real world, most of the time, workflow should be implemented as a workflow service hosted in IIS7 or AppFabric.

AppFabric is an IIS7 extension that includes many tools to help us host a workflow service. AppFabric is to workflow service like IIS7 is to ASP.NET website. However, we can run a workflow service in IIS7 without AppFabric installed. Although AppFabric is powerful, we need to spend some time to learn it. For more information about AppFabric, you can check this link: http://msdn.microsoft.com/appfabric.

Hosting a workflow service in IIS7

The process of sending an e-mail would consume some time—maybe a few seconds or even minutes. It would be a waste of time and resources for our applications to stop and wait for an e-mail sending action to complete. Because sending e-mail is time-consuming, a better design is to strip this feature out as an independent WCF workflow service and host that service in IIS7.

Getting ready

We need the `SendEmailActivity` activity to send an e-mail. We can check this activity in *Chapter 5, Custom Activities*.

How to do it...

1. **Create a WCF workflow service application**:

   Create a WCF workflow service application and name it `HostingWorkflowServiceInIIS7`.

   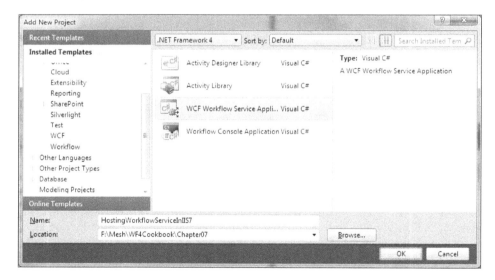

2. **Add SendEmailActivity to the toolbox**:

   In the **Toolbox** tab, right-click and select **Choose Items**. In the opening dialog, click **Browse** and navigate to the `ActivityLibrary.dll` from the sample code of `chapter05`. Next, check `SendEmailActivity`:

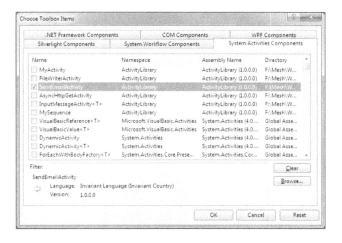

Click **OK**. We will find `SendEmailActivity` in the toolbox:

3. **Create a SendEmail workflow service**:

    i. Delete `Service1.xamlx`, which is created by default, and add a new WCF workflow service to the project. Name it `SendEmailService.xamlx`. Drag a `TransactedReceiveScope` activity to the design panel, click the **Variables** button, and create a variable named `emailMessage`:

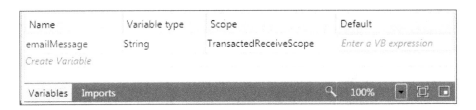

ii. Drag a `Receive` activity to the **Request** box of
    `TransactedReceiveScope`. Set the `OperationName` to `SendEmail`.
    Click the **Content Definition** link to create a parameter as shown here:

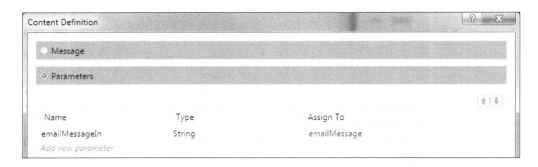

iii. Assign `ISendEmailService` to the `ServiceContractName` property.
    Check the `CanCreateInstance` property.

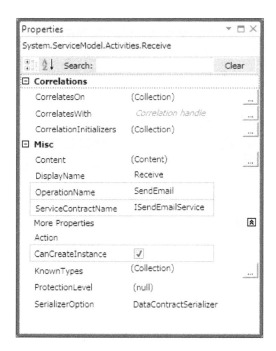

iv. Next, drag `SendEmailActivity` to the body of
    `TransactedReceiveScope`.

v.   Assign the following properties to `SendEmailActivity`:

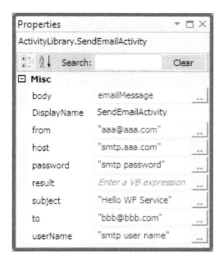

vi. The final workflow will look as shown in the following screenshot:

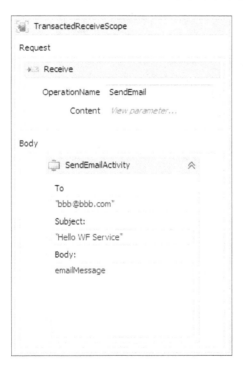

4. **Create a website in IIS7 for this WF service**:

In IIS7 Manager Console, create a website and assign the website's physical path to the project folder of `HostingWorkflowServiceInIIS7`. Assign it a new port number. By default, an ASP.NET application will run under the built-in network service account (or `ApplicationPoolIdentity` in IIS7.5). This account has the most limited permissions. For testing, we can shift the application pool's identity to an administrator account.

We should be able to find the following module and handlers in IIS7:

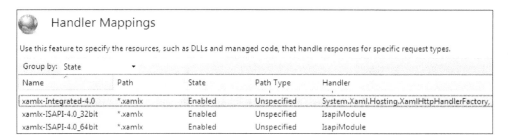

If we cannot, then we should reinstall .NET framework 4.0 or repair it. Here are the repair commands:

Repair command for 32-bit:

```
.NET Framework 4 Full (32-bit) - silent repair
%windir%\Microsoft.NET\Framework\v4.0.30319\SetupCache\Client\
setup.exe /repair /x86 /x64 /ia64 /parameterfolder Client /q /
norestart
```

Repair command for 64-bit:

```
.NET Framework 4 Full (64-bit) - silent repair
%windir%\Microsoft.NET\Framework64\v4.0.30319\SetupCache\Client\
setup.exe /repair /x86 /x64 /ia64 /parameterfolder Client /q /
norestart
```

5. **Use WCFTestClient.exe to test the WCF service**:

   Usually, we can find the `WCFTestClient.exe` tool in `C:\Program Files (x86)\ Microsoft Visual Studio 10.0\Common7\IDE`.

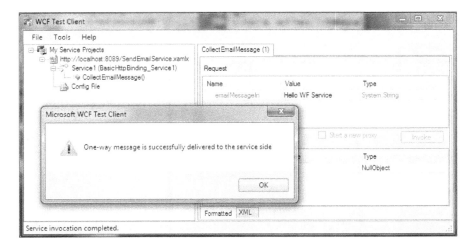

We just need to open our mail. A new mail with subject **Hello WF Service** indicates that we have created and hosted the WF service successfully.

How it works...

Simply put, once we have set up the IIS7, we need to copy all the workflow service project files and folders to the IIS application folder and the workflow service will just work.

There's more

We can also host a WF4 service in IIS6 once we have installed .NET framework 4.0. Running a WF4 service in IIS6 is not recommended.

See also

> ▶ *To host workflow service in console application, we need to refer to the Receiving and replying to a WCF message section in Chapter 3, Messaging and Transaction.*

Hosting workflow in ASP.NET

In this task, we will create an e-mail sending workflow and run it in an ASP.NET site.

Getting ready

We need an e-mail sending workflow service hosted in IIS7. We can refer to the previous section, *Hosting a workflow service in IIS7*, in this chapter.

How to do it...

1. **Create an ASP.NET4 web application**:

   Create an ASP.NET4 web application and name it `HostingWorkflowInASPNET`. Because we are going to host WF4 workflow in this website, we have to make sure it is an ASP.NET4 website. To check the version, right-click the project name `HostingWorkflowInASPNET` and select **Properties**.

2. **Author a Workflow**:

   i.   Add an activity to the website and name it `Workflow.xaml`.

   Author the workflow as follows:

ii.   Set the properties for **SendEmail1**:

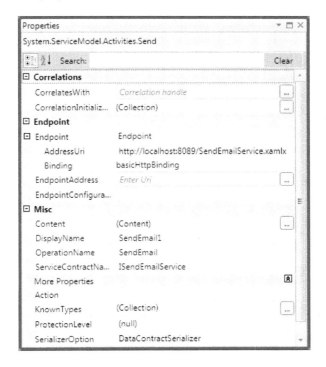

iii.   Set the parameters for **SendEmail1**:

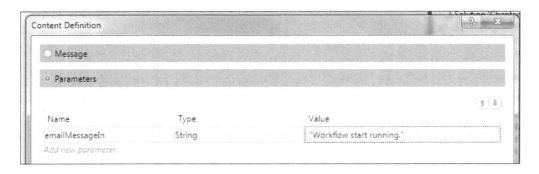

iv.   Set the properties of **SendEmail2**. The only difference as compared to SendEmail1 is the **DisplayName**.

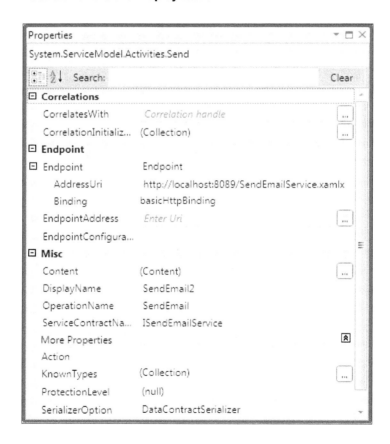

v.   Set the parameters for **SendEmail2**:

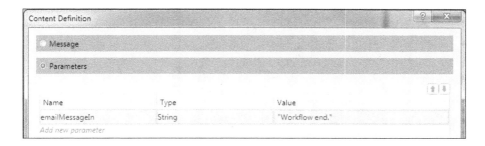

3.   **Alter the Default.aspx page**:

Add a Button control to the `Default.aspx` page:

```
<%@ Page Title="Home Page"
        Language="C#"
        MasterPageFile="~/Site.master"
        AutoEventWireup="true"
        CodeBehind="Default.aspx.cs"
        Inherits="HostingWorkflowInASPNET._Default" %>
<asp:Content ID="HeaderContent" runat="server"
        ContentPlaceHolderID="HeadContent">
</asp:Content>
<asp:Content ID="BodyContent" runat="server"
        ContentPlaceHolderID="MainContent">
    <p>
        <asp:Button ID="Button1" runat="server"
                Text="Start a workflow"
                onclick="Button1_Click" />
    </p>
</asp:Content>
```

Add this code to the button event handler in `Default.aspx.cs`:

```
using System;
using System.Activities;
using System.Threading;
namespace HostingWorkflowInASPNET {
    public partial class _Default : System.Web.UI.Page {
        protected void Page_Load(object sender, EventArgs e) {
        }
        protected void Button1_Click(object sender, EventArgs e) {
```

```
                    AutoResetEvent waitHandler = new
                                        AutoResetEvent(false);
                    WorkflowApplication wfApp =
                        new WorkflowApplication(new Workflow());
                    wfApp.Unloaded = (workflowApplicationEventArgs) => {
                        waitHandler.Set();
                    };
                    wfApp.Run();
                    waitHandler.WaitOne();
                }
            }
        }
```

4. **Run it**:

    Build the website and browse to the default page:

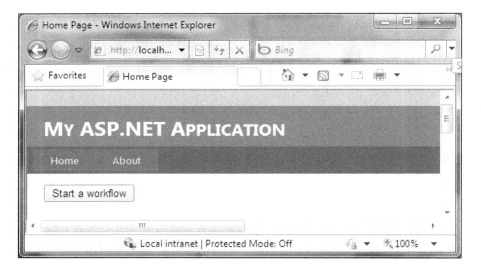

    Click the **Start a workflow** button to start a workflow. Open your e-mail client. Two mails with subject **Hello WF Service** indicate we have finished this task successfully.

How it works...

We can treat a WF4 workflow as a managed .NET object and it can run in any .NET framework 4.0 application. If we have experience with WF3/3.5, we may still remember that we had to schedule the workflow instance in an ASP.NET application. In WF4, a `WorkflowApplication` workflow instance runs in an independent .NET thread. No special workflow schedule is needed.

There's more

As I have stated in the introduction of this chapter, usually we don't run a workflow instance in an ASP.NET page directly; instead, we call a WF4 service in page events. For example, in this task, we can call the WF4 service using pure .NET code by following these steps:

1. Use `Svcutil.exe` to generate the proxy code and configuration code. Usually, if we have installed .NET 4.0 framework, we can find this `Svcutil.exe` in `C:\Program Files (x86)\Microsoft SDKs\Windows\v7.0A\Bin` or `C:\Program Files\Microsoft SDKs\Windows\v7.0A\Bin`.

2. In a command window, navigate to the `svcutil.exe` folder using the following command:

   cd C:\Program Files (x86)\Microsoft SDKs\Windows\v7.0A\Bin

3. Input the following command:

   svcutil.exe /language:cs /out:c:\GeneratedProxy.cs /config:c:\app. config http://localhost:8089/SendEmailService.xamlx.

   Press the *Enter* key, and we will find the `GeneratedProxy.cs` and `app.config` files in `C:\`.

4. Add `GeneratedProxy.cs` to our ASP.NET web application.

5. Open the `app.config` file and copy the following configuration code into the `web.config` file of the ASP.NET web application right below the `<configuration>` node:

```
<system.serviceModel>
        <bindings>
            <basicHttpBinding>
                <binding name="BasicHttpBinding_ISendEmailService"
closeTimeout="00:01:00"
                    openTimeout="00:01:00"
receiveTimeout="00:10:00" sendTimeout="00:01:00"
                    allowCookies="false"
bypassProxyOnLocal="false" hostNameComparisonMode="StrongWildcard"
                    maxBufferSize="65536"
maxBufferPoolSize="524288" maxReceivedMessageSize="65536"
```

```
                              messageEncoding="Text" textEncoding="utf-8"
        transferMode="Buffered"
                              useDefaultWebProxy="true">
                              <readerQuotas maxDepth="32"
        maxStringContentLength="8192" maxArrayLength="16384"
                                  maxBytesPerRead="4096"
        maxNameTableCharCount="16384" />
                              <security mode="None">
                                   <transport clientCredentialType="None"
        proxyCredentialType="None"
                                        realm="">
                                        <extendedProtectionPolicy
        policyEnforcement="Never" />
                                   </transport>
                                   <message clientCredentialType="UserName"
        algorithmSuite="Default" />
                              </security>
                         </binding>
                    </basicHttpBinding>
               </bindings>
               <client>
                    <endpoint address="http://localhost:8089/
        SendEmailService.xamlx"
                         binding="basicHttpBinding" bindingConfiguration="B
        asicHttpBinding_ISendEmailService"
                         contract="ISendEmailService"
        name="BasicHttpBinding_ISendEmailService" />
               </client>
        </system.serviceModel>
```

6. Use the following code to call the workflow service:

```
SendEmailServiceClient sesc = new SendEmailServiceClient();
sesc.SendEmail("message");
```

Hosting workflow in WPF

In this task, we will create a workflow running in a WPF application.

How to do it...

1. **Create a WPF project**:

   Create a WPF project and name it `HostingWorkflowInWPF`.

2. **Create a workflow**:

   Add a workflow to the project named `AdditionWorkflow.xaml` and author a workflow like this:

3. **Create a WPF window**:

   Open the default created WPF file `MainWindow.xaml`. Alter its contents to:

```
<Window x:Class="HostingWorkflowInWPF.MainWindow"
        xmlns="http://schemas.microsoft.com/winfx/2006/xaml/
                                        presentation"
        xmlns:x="http://schemas.microsoft.com/winfx/2006/xaml"
        Title="MainWindow" Height="160" Width="200">
    <Grid Width="180" HorizontalAlignment="Left"
        VerticalAlignment="Top" Height="124">
        <Label Content="x:" Width="20"
            HorizontalAlignment="Left" Name="LabelX"
            Margin="0,2,0,0" VerticalAlignment="Top" />
        <TextBox Name="textBoxX" Width="80"
            Height="20" VerticalAlignment="Top"
            HorizontalAlignment="Left" Margin="52,4,0,0" />
```

```
        <Label Content="y:" HorizontalAlignment="Left"
                Margin="0,26,0,0" Name="labelY"
                Width="20" Height="30"
                VerticalAlignment="Top" />
        <TextBox Height="20" HorizontalAlignment="Left"
                Margin="52,28,0,0" Name="textBoxY"
                VerticalAlignment="Top" Width="80" />
        <Button Content="Adding" Height="23"
                HorizontalAlignment="Left" Margin="52,54,0,0"
                Name="buttonAdding" VerticalAlignment="Top"
                Width="75" Click="buttonAdding_Click" />
        <Label Content="result:" Height="28"
                HorizontalAlignment="Left" Margin="0,83,0,0"
                Name="labelResult" VerticalAlignment="Top" />
        <Label Height="28" HorizontalAlignment="Left"
                Margin="52,83,0,0" Name="labelResultValue"
                VerticalAlignment="Top" />
    </Grid>
</Window>
```

We can see this in the WPF window designer:

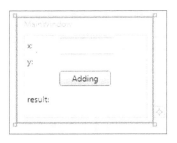

Double-click the **Adding** button, and add code to the button event handler. The final
`MainWindow.xaml.cs` code will be:

```
using System.Windows;
using System.Threading;
using System.Activities;
using System;
namespace HostingWorkflowInWPF {
    public partial class MainWindow : Window {
        public MainWindow() {
            InitializeComponent();
        }
```

```
private void buttonAdding_Click(object sender, RoutedEventArgs e)
{
        AutoResetEvent waitHandler = new
AutoResetEvent(false);
        string result = "";
        AdditionWorkflow addwf = new AdditionWorkflow {
            x = new InArgument<Int32>(Int32.
                                    Parse(textBoxX.Text)),
            y = new InArgument<Int32>(Int32.
                                    Parse(textBoxY.Text))
        };
        WorkflowApplication wfApp = new
                            WorkflowApplication(addwf);
        wfApp.Completed =
        (workflowApplicationCompletedEventArgs) => {
            result = workflowApplicationCompletedEventArgs.
                    Outputs["result"].ToString();
        };
        wfApp.Unloaded = (workflowApplicationEventArgs) => {
                        waitHandler.Set(); };
        wfApp.Run();
        waitHandler.WaitOne();
        labelResultValue.Content = result;
    }
  }
}
```

4. **Run it**:

   Set this project as StartUp project. Press *Ctrl+F5* to run the workflow without debugging. Now we shall see the following:

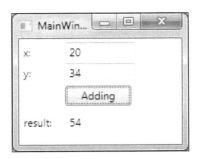

This task is only for the purpose of concept demonstration. In a real application, it is not a good idea to host a workflow in a WPF application. It would be better to host the workflow in IIS and call it in the WPF application like we did in the previous ASP.NET web application.

Hosting workflow in a Windows Form

In this task we will create a workflow running in a Windows Form application.

How to do it...

1. **Create a Windows Form project**:

   Create a Windows Form project and name it `HostingWorkflowInWinForm`.

2. **Create a workflow**:

   Add a workflow to the project and call it `AdditionWorkflow.xaml`. Author the workflow like this:

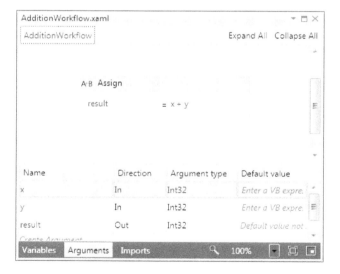

3. **Create a Windows Form**.

   Open the default created `Form1.cs` file and alter it to:

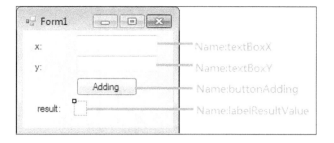

Double-click the **Adding** button and add code to the button event handler. The final code will be:

```
using System;
using System.Windows.Forms;
using System.Threading;
using System.Activities;
namespace HostingWorkflowInWinForm {
public partial class Form1 : Form {
public Form1() {
InitializeComponent();
}
private void buttonAdding_Click(object sender,
    EventArgse) {
AutoResetEventwaitHandler =
newAutoResetEvent(false);
string result = "";
AdditionWorkflowaddwf =
new AdditionWorkflow {
x = new InArgument<Int32>(
        Int32.Parse(textBoxX.Text.ToString())),
    y = new InArgument<Int32>(
        Int32.Parse(textBoxY.Text.ToString()))
    };
WorkflowApplicationwfApp =
newWorkflowApplication(addwf);
wfApp.Completed =
(workflowApplicationCompletedEventArgs) => {
result = workflowApplicationCompletedEventArgs.Outputs["result"].
ToString();
};
wfApp.Unloaded = (workflowApplicationEventArgs) => {
waitHandler.Set();
};
wfApp.Run();
```

```
                    waitHandler.WaitOne();
                    labelResultValue.Text = result;
            }
        }
    }
```

4. **Run it**:

   Set this project as StartUp project and press *Ctrl+F5* to run this project without debugging. We shall see the following:

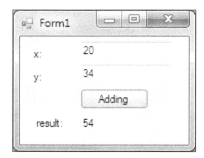

How it works...

This task is only for the purpose of concept demonstration. In a real application, it is not a good idea to host a workflow in a Windows Form application. It would be better to host the workflow in IIS and call it from a Win Form application like we did in the previous ASP.NET web application.

8
Custom Workflow Designer

In this chapter, we will cover:

- ▶ Implementing designer layout
- ▶ Implementing Toolbox, Workflow Designer, and Property Inspector views
- ▶ Implementing New Workflow and Load Workflow events
- ▶ Implementing Save and Save As events
- ▶ Implementing XAML Workflow Tab and Run events
- ▶ Implementing visual tracking

Introduction

Sometimes, workflow users are non-developers who may not have installed Visual Studio 2010. These users need the ability to create and/or modify workflow definitions with designer support for things such as dragging and dropping of activities. WF4 provides a set of WPF classes that we can reference and use to create our own custom workflow designer, allowing for creating of rich administration tools for our workflow solutions.

There are several important classes involved in creating custom hosted workflow designers.

- ▶ `System.Activities.Presentation.WorkflowDesigner`:

  `WorkflowDesigner` provides a designer canvas that renders the visual workflow model. `WorklfowDesigner.View` represents the designer canvas. We can get the property inspector view from `WorkflowDesigner.PropertyInspectorView`.

▶ System.Activities.Presentation.ToolboxControl

ToolboxControl renders categorized workflow activities in the toolbox. We can use System.Activities.Presentation.Toolbox.ToolboxCategory to create an activity category, and use System.Activities.Presentation.Toolbox.ToolboxItemWrapper to wrap a workflow activity. We can display an activities tree in Toolbox by adding ToolboxItemWrapper objects to a ToolboxCategory object and then adding the ToolboxCategory object to the ToolboxControl object's Categories collection.

As WF4 workflow designer is based on WPF, familiarity with some basic WPF knowledge will be helpful to gain more understanding.

The goal of this chapter is creating a workflow designer. Every task will build one part of it and each task will be the base for the next task.

Implementing designer layout

In this task, we will create a WF4 designer layout window. This is just a WPF window. When we finish this task, we will have built a designer window. Functions will be added to the window in the following tasks.

How to do it...

1. **Create a WPF Application project**:

   Open a new Visual Studio 2010 instance and create a new WPF Application project. Name the project WF4Designer.

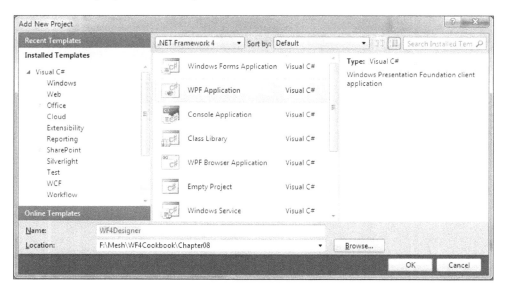

Add the following three assembly references to the project: `System.Activities`, `System.Activities.Core.Presentation`, and `System.Activities. Presentation`.

2. **Create XAML layout code**:

Open the `MainWindow.xaml` file, which is created by default. Fill the file with XAML code as follows:

```xml
<Window x:Class="WF4Designer.MainWindow"
        xmlns="http://schemas.microsoft.com/winfx/2006/xaml/
                                              presentation"
        xmlns:x="http://schemas.microsoft.com/winfx/2006/xaml"
        Title="MainWindow" Height="600" Width="800">
    <Grid>
        <Grid.RowDefinitions>
            <RowDefinition Height="25" />
            <RowDefinition Height="*" />
        </Grid.RowDefinitions>
        <Grid.ColumnDefinitions>
            <ColumnDefinition Width="200" />
            <ColumnDefinition Width="*" />
            <ColumnDefinition Width="200"/>
        </Grid.ColumnDefinitions>
        <GridSplitter   HorizontalAlignment="Right"
                        VerticalAlignment="Stretch"
                        Width="5"
                        Grid.Column="0"
                        Grid.Row="1" />
        <GridSplitter   HorizontalAlignment="Left"
                        VerticalAlignment="Stretch"
                        Width="5"
                        Grid.Column="2"
                        Grid.Row="1" />
        <StackPanel Grid.ColumnSpan="3">
            <Menu Height="25"
                  VerticalAlignment="Top">
                <MenuItem Header="File">
                    <MenuItem Header="New Workflow"
                            Click="MenuItem_Click_NewWorkflow"/>
                    <MenuItem Header="Load Workflow"
                            Click="MenuItem_Click_
LoadWorkflow"/>
```

```xml
                                    <Separator />
                                    <MenuItem Header="Save"
                                            Click="MenuItem_Click_Save"/>
                                    <MenuItem Header="Save As"
                                            Click="MenuItem_Click_SaveAs"/>
                            </MenuItem>
                            <MenuItem Header="Test">
                                    <MenuItem Header="Run"
                                            Click="MenuItem_Click_RunWorkflow"/>
                            </MenuItem>
                    </Menu>
            </StackPanel>
            <TabControl HorizontalAlignment="Stretch"
                        VerticalAlignment="Stretch"
                        Margin="0,0,5,0"
                        Grid.Column="0"
                        Grid.Row="1">
                    <TabItem Header="Toolbox">
                        <ContentControl Name="toolboxPanel"/>
                    </TabItem>
            </TabControl>
            <TabControl HorizontalAlignment="Stretch"
                        VerticalAlignment="Stretch"
                        Margin="0,0,0,0"
                        Grid.Column="1"
                        Grid.Row="1">
                    <TabItem Header="WorkflowDesinger">
                        <ContentControl Name="workflowDesignerPanel"/>
                    </TabItem>
                    <TabItem Header="XAML workflow"
                            GotFocus="TabItem_GotFocus_RefreshXamlBox" >
                        <TextBox Name="xamlTextBox"
                                AcceptsReturn="True"
                                HorizontalScrollBarVisibility="Auto"
                                VerticalScrollBarVisibility="Auto">
                                                        </TextBox>
                    </TabItem>
            </TabControl>
            <TabControl HorizontalAlignment="Stretch"
                        VerticalAlignment="Stretch"
                        Margin="5,0,0,0"
```

```
                        Grid.Column="2"
                        Grid.Row="1">
                <TabItem Header="WorkflowProperty">
                    <ContentControl Name="WorkflowPropertyPanel"/>
                </TabItem>
            </TabControl>
        </Grid>
    </Window>
```

3. **Add empty event handlers to the code-behind file**:

   Open the `MainWindow.xaml.cs` file and alter its code as follows:

```csharp
using System.Windows;
namespace WF4Designer {
    public partial class MainWindow : Window {
        public MainWindow() {
            InitializeComponent();
        }
        private void MenuItem_Click_NewWorkflow(object sender,
                                    RoutedEventArgs e)
        {
        }
        private void MenuItem_Click_LoadWorkflow(object sender,
                                    RoutedEventArgs e)
        {
        }
        private void MenuItem_Click_Save(object sender,
                                        RoutedEventArgs e)
        {
        }
        private void MenuItem_Click_SaveAs(object sender,
                                        RoutedEventArgs e)
        {
        }
        private void MenuItem_Click_RunWorkflow(object sender,
                                        RoutedEventArgs e)
        {
        }
        private void TabItem_GotFocus_RefreshXamlBox(object
                                    sender, RoutedEventArgs e)
        {
        }
    }
}
```

4. **Build and run it**:

   Press *Ctrl+F5* to run the project. We shall see:

How it works...

In the XAML code, the `GridSplitter` enables us to resize three columns without changing the dimensions of the grid.

See also

▶ *To find more info about WPF layout, please check WPF MSDN document, available at* `http://msdn.microsoft.com/en-us/library/ms745058.aspx`.

Implementing Toolbox, Workflow Designer, and Property Inspector views

In this task we will render the Toolbox, Workflow Designer View, and Property Inspector View to their corresponding content panel.

Getting ready

Before we begin this task, we should have completed that task of *implementing designer layout*.

How to do it...

1. **Open the workflow designer project**:

   Open the workflow designer project we created in the previous task.

2. **Add code to the designer**:

   Open the designer's backend CS code file and alter the code as following. Code in bold style is the new added code.

```
using System.Windows;
using System.Activities.Presentation;
using System.Activities.Presentation.Toolbox;
using System.Activities.Statements;

namespace WF4Designer {
    public partial class MainWindow : Window {
        public MainWindow() {
            InitializeComponent();
            this.AddDesigner();
            this.AddToolBox();
            this.AddPropertyInspector();
        }

        WorkflowDesigner wd = null;
        private void AddDesigner() {
            this.wd = new WorkflowDesigner();
            this.workflowDesignerPanel.Content = wd.View;
        }

        private void AddToolBox() {
            ToolboxControl tc = GetToolboxControl();
            this.toolboxPanel.Content = tc;
        }

        private ToolboxControl GetToolboxControl() {
            ToolboxControl toolboxControl = new ToolboxControl();
            ToolboxCategory toolboxCategory =
                    new ToolboxCategory("Activities");
            ToolboxItemWrapper sequence =
                    new ToolboxItemWrapper(typeof(Sequence));
            ToolboxItemWrapper writeLine =
                    new ToolboxItemWrapper(typeof(WriteLine));
            toolboxCategory.Add(sequence);
            toolboxCategory.Add(writeLine);
            toolboxControl.Categories.Add(toolboxCategory);
            return toolboxControl;
        }

        private void AddPropertyInspector() {
            if (wd == null)
                return;
            this.WorkflowPropertyPanel.Content = wd.PropertyInspec
torView;
        }
```

```
                private void MenuItem_Click_NewWorkflow(object sender,
                                                        RoutedEventArgs e)
                {
                }
                private void MenuItem_Click_LoadWorkflow(object sender,
                                                        RoutedEventArgs e)
                {
                }
                private void MenuItem_Click_Save(object sender,
                                                        RoutedEventArgs e)
                {
                }
                private void MenuItem_Click_SaveAs(object sender,
                                                        RoutedEventArgs e)
                {
                }
                private void MenuItem_Click_RunWorkflow(object sender,
                                                        RoutedEventArgs e)
                {
                }
                private void TabItem_GotFocus_RefreshXamlBox(object
                                                   sender, RoutedEventArgs e)
                {
                }
        }
    }
```

3. **Run it**:

    Press *Ctrl+F5* to run it. We will see the following:

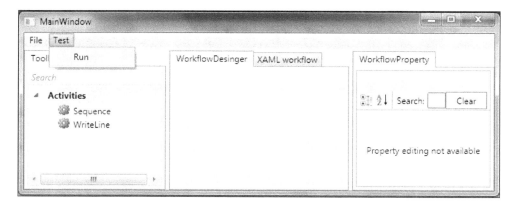

How it works...

Using the following code, we construct a complete Toolbox Control:

```
ToolboxControltoolboxControl = new ToolboxControl();
ToolboxCategorytoolboxCategory =
        new ToolboxCategory("Activities");
ToolboxItemWrapper sequence =
        new ToolboxItemWrapper(type of(Sequence));
ToolboxItemWrapperwriteLine =
        new ToolboxItemWrapper(type of(WriteLine));
toolboxCategory.Add(sequence);
toolboxCategory.Add(writeLine);
toolboxControl.Categories.Add(toolboxCategory);
```

Using the following code, we render the workflow designer view to the designer panel:

```
this.wd = new WorkflowDesigner();
this.workflowDesignerPanel.Content = wd.View;
```

And using the following code, we render the property view to the property panel:

```
this.WorkflowPropertyPanel.Content = wd.PropertyInspectorView;
```

Implementing New Workflow and Load Workflow events

In this task, we will give our workflow designer the ability to create new workflows and load workflow from XAML files.

Getting ready

Before we begin this task, we must complete the previous task: _Implementing Toolbox, Workflow Designer, and Property Inspector views_.

How to do it...

1. **Open the workflow designer project**:

   Open the workflow designer project we created in the previous task.

2. **Create a new empty workflow as an empty workflow template**:

Click on the **Show All Files** button and navigate to the project's `bin\Debug` folder.

Create a new XAML file named `WFTemplate.xaml`. Fill the file with the following XAML code:

```
<Activity mc:Ignorable="sap"
          x:Class="WFTemplate"
          sap:VirtualizedContainerService.HintSize="240,240"
          mva:VisualBasic.Settings="Assembly references and
imported namespaces for internal implementation"
          xmlns="http://schemas.microsoft.com/netfx/2009/xaml/
                 activities"
          xmlns:mc="http://schemas.openxmlformats.org/markup-
compatibility/2006"
          xmlns:mv="clr-namespace:Microsoft.
VisualBasic;assembly=System"
          xmlns:mva="clr-namespace:Microsoft.VisualBasic.
Activities;assembly=System.Activities"
          xmlns:s="clr-namespace:System;assembly=mscorlib"
          xmlns:s1="clr-namespace:System;assembly=System"
          xmlns:s2="clr-namespace:System;assembly=System.Xml"
          xmlns:s3="clr-namespace:System;assembly=System.Core"
          xmlns:sap="http://schemas.microsoft.com/netfx/2009/xaml/
activities/presentation"
          xmlns:scg="clr-namespace:System.Collections.
Generic;assembly=System"
          xmlns:scg1="clr-namespace:System.Collections.
Generic;assembly=System.ServiceModel"
```

```
        xmlns:scg2="clr-namespace:System.Collections.
Generic;assembly=System.Core"
        xmlns:scg3="clr-namespace:System.Collections.
Generic;assembly=mscorlib"
        xmlns:sd="clr-namespace:System.Data;assembly=System.
                Data"
        xmlns:sl="clr-namespace:System.Linq;assembly=System.
                Core"
        xmlns:st="clr-namespace:System.Text;assembly=mscorlib"
        xmlns:x="http://schemas.microsoft.com/winfx/2006/xaml"
/>
```

If we don't want to type in the code, we can create a new activity and copy this `WFTemplate.xaml` file to the project's `bin\Debug` folder.

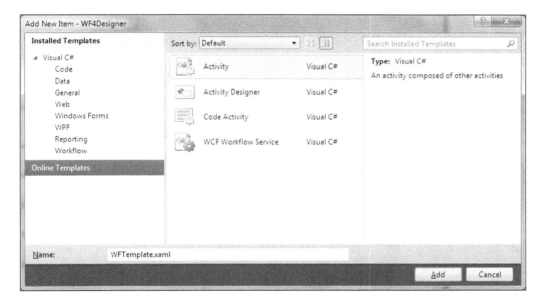

Open the file with XML Editor and make sure the `x:Class` property is set to `WFTemplate`.

```
x:Class="WFTemplate"
```

3. **Add code to the designer**:

   Open the designer's backend CS code file—`MainWindow.xaml.cs`—and alter the code as following:

```
using System;
using System.Windows;
```

```
using System.Windows.Controls;
using System.Activities.Presentation;
using System.Activities.Presentation.Toolbox;
using System.Activities.Statements;
using System.Activities.Presentation.View;
using System.Activities.Core.Presentation;

namespace WF4Designer {
    public partial class MainWindow : Window {
        public MainWindow() {
            InitializeComponent();
            (new DesignerMetadata()).Register();//Registers the
             runtime metadata.
            this.AddDesigner();
            this.AddToolBox();
            this.AddPropertyInspector();
        }

        WorkflowDesigner wd = null;
        private void AddDesigner() {
            this.wd = new WorkflowDesigner();
            this.workflowDesignerPanel.Content = wd.View;
        }

        private void AddToolBox() {
            ToolboxControl tc = GetToolboxControl();
            this.toolboxPanel.Content = tc;
        }

        private ToolboxControl GetToolboxControl() {
            ToolboxControl toolboxControl = new ToolboxControl();
            ToolboxCategory toolboxCategory =
                        new ToolboxCategory("Activities");
            ToolboxItemWrapper sequence =
                        new ToolboxItemWrapper(typeof(Sequence));
            ToolboxItemWrapper writeLine =
                        new ToolboxItemWrapper(typeof(WriteLine));
            toolboxCategory.Add(sequence);
            toolboxCategory.Add(writeLine);
            toolboxControl.Categories.Add(toolboxCategory);
            return toolboxControl;
        }
```

```
        private void AddPropertyInspector() {
            if (wd == null)
return;
this.WorkflowPropertyPanel.Content =
wd.PropertyInspectorView;
}
stringworkflowFilePathName = "temp.xaml";
private void LoadWorkflowFromFile(string fileName) {
workflowFilePathName = fileName;
workflowDesignerPanel.Content = null;
WorkflowPropertyPanel.Content = null;
wd = new WorkflowDesigner();
wd.Load(workflowFilePathName);
DesignerViewdesignerView =
        wd.Context.Services.GetService<DesignerView>();
designerView.WorkflowShellBarItemVisibility =
ShellBarItemVisibility.Arguments |
ShellBarItemVisibility.Imports|
ShellBarItemVisibility.MiniMap|
ShellBarItemVisibility.Variables|
ShellBarItemVisibility.Zoom;
workflowDesignerPanel.Content = wd.View;
WorkflowPropertyPanel.Content =wd.PropertyInspectorView;
}
private void MenuItem_Click_NewWorkflow(object sender,
RoutedEventArgs e) {
workflowFilePathName = @"WFTemplate.xaml";
LoadWorkflowFromFile(workflowFilePathName);
workflowFilePathName = "temp.xaml";
}
private void MenuItem_Click_LoadWorkflow(object sender,
RoutedEventArgs e) {
Microsoft.Win32.OpenFileDialog openFileDialog=
new Microsoft.Win32.OpenFileDialog();
if(openFileDialog.ShowDialog(this).Value) {
workflowFilePathName = openFileDialog.FileName;
```

```
                    LoadWorkflowFromFile(workflowFilePathName);
              }
       }
       private void MenuItem_Click_Save(object sender,
                                        RoutedEventArgs e)
       {
       }
       private void MenuItem_Click_SaveAs(object sender,
                                          RoutedEventArgs e)
       {
       }
       private void MenuItem_Click_RunWorkflow(object sender,
                                               RoutedEventArgs e)
       {
       }
       private void TabItem_GotFocus_RefreshXamlBox(object
                                      sender, RoutedEventArgs e)
       {
       }
    }
}
```

3. **Run it**:

    Press *Ctrl+F5* to run the workflow designer. Now, we can create a new workflow or load an XAML workflow from file by using this workflow designer.

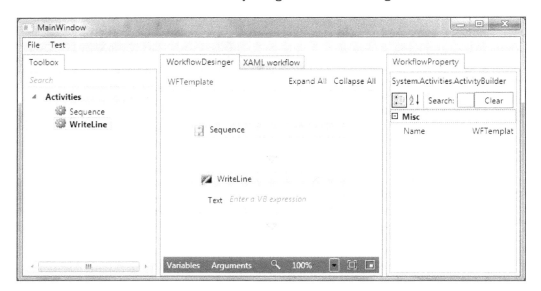

How it works...

The process of creating a new workflow is actually similar to loading an empty workflow from file.

```
wd.Load(workflowFilePathName);
```

Now consider this code:

```
DesignerViewdesignerView =
wd.Context.Services. GetService<DesignerView>();
designerView.WorkflowShellBarItemVisibility =
ShellBarItemVisibility.Arguments|
ShellBarItemVisibility.Imports|
ShellBarItemVisibility.MiniMap|
ShellBarItemVisibility.Variables|
ShellBarItemVisibility.Zoom;
```

Using this code, we enable the following buttons in the bottom of the designer:

If we want to show all items, we can use the following code statement:

```
designerView.WorkflowShellBarItemVisibility = ShellBarItemVisibility.
All;
```

Implementing Save and Save As events

In this task, we will give our workflow designer the ability to save workflow into an XAML file.

Getting ready

Before we begin this task, we must complete the previous task: *Implementing New Workflow and Load Workflow events*.

How to do it...

1. **Open the workflow designer project**:

    Open the workflow designer project we created in the previous task.

2. **Add code to the designer**:

Open the designer's backend CS code file and add code for the following three methods: Save method, MenuItem_Click_Save method, and MenuItem_Click_SaveAs method:

```
private void Save() {
if (workflowFilePathName == "temp.xaml") {
Microsoft.Win32.SaveFileDialog saveFileDialog =
 new Microsoft.Win32.SaveFileDialog();
if (saveFileDialog.ShowDialog(this).Value) {
workflowFilePathName = saveFileDialog.FileName;
wd.Save(workflowFilePathName);
MessageBox.Show("Save Ok");
this.Title = "Workflow Designer - " + workflowFilePathName;
} else {
return;
}
} else {
wd.Save(workflowFilePathName);
MessageBox.Show("Save Ok");
}
LoadWorkflowFromFile(workflowFilePathName);
}
private void MenuItem_Click_Save(object sender, RoutedEventArgs e)
{
Save();
}
private void MenuItem_Click_SaveAs(object sender, RoutedEventArgs
e) {
Microsoft.Win32.SaveFileDialog saveFileDialog =
 new Microsoft. Win32.SaveFileDialog();
if (saveFileDialog.ShowDialog(this).Value) {
workflowFilePathName = saveFileDialog.FileName;
wd.Save(workflowFilePathName);
MessageBox.Show("Save Ok");
this.Title =
"Workflow Designer - " + workflowFilePathName;
}
}
```

3. **Run it:**

   Press *Ctrl+F5* to run the workflow designer. We can now save the newly created workflow or save our workflow as a new file.

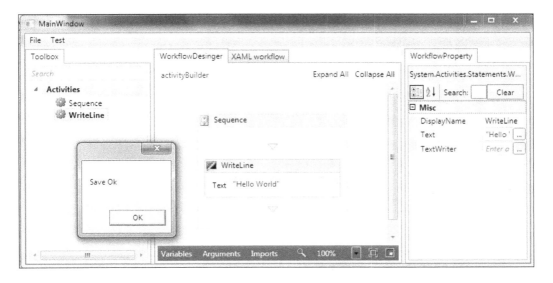

How it works...

In this task, we added three methods to the `MainWindow` class (`MainWindow.xaml.cs`). The `Save` method can save workflow as an XAML string into a file. The following code statement does the actual saving job:

```
wd.Save(workflowFilePathName);
```

The `MenuItem_Click_Save` method is the save event handler; this method simply calls the `Save` method.

The `MenuItem_Click_SaveAs` method can save workflow as an XAML string into a new file.

Implementing XAML Workflow Tab and Run events

In this task, our workflow designer will have the ability to run workflow so that we can test our workflow when we are editing.

Getting ready

Before we begin this task, we must have completed the previous task: *Implementing Save and Save As events*.

How to do it...

1. **Open the workflow designer project**:

   Open the workflow designer project we created in the previous task.

2. **Add code to the designer**:

   Open the designer's backend CS code file, `MainWindow.xaml.cs`, and create a new method `GetActivity`. Then add code to the `TabItem_GotFocus_RefreshXamlBox` method and the `MenuItem_Click_RunWorkflow` method:

```
Activity GetActivity() {
wd.Flush();
System.IO.StringReaderstringReader =
new System. IO.StringReader(wd.Text);
Activity root =
System.Activities.XamlIntegration.
ActivityXamlServices.Load(stringReader) as Activity;
return root;
}
private void MenuItem_Click_RunWorkflow(object sender,
RoutedEventArgs e) {
Save();
Activity activity = GetActivity();
WorkflowApplicationwfApp =
 new WorkflowApplication(activity);
wfApp.Run();
        }
private void TabItem_GotFocus_RefreshXamlBox(object sender,
RoutedEventArgs e) {
if (wd.Text != null) {
wd.Flush();
xamlTextBox.Text = wd.Text;
}
}
```

   As we are using the Activity class in this task, we need to add an assembly reference to `System.Activities` and add `using System.Activities` in the top of the class file.

3. **Run it**:

Right-click on the project name and select **Properties**. Then, change the project type from **Windows Application** to **Console Application** for us to be able to see the command output from the `WriteLine` activity.

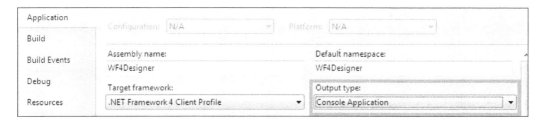

Press *Ctrl+F5* to run the workflow designer.

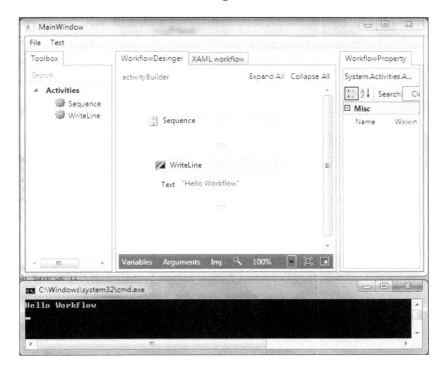

How it works...

In the `GetActivity` method, the code statement `wd.Flush();` saves the current state of the workflow to the `Text` property, so that we can use `wd.Text` to get the current workflow's XAML string. Using the following code statement:

```
System.IO.StringReader stringReader = new System.IO.StringReader(wd.
Text);
```

we created a `StringReader` object for the workflow XAML string (`wd.Text`). Using the following code statement:

```
Activity root = System.Activities.XamlIntegration.
ActivityXamlServices.Load(stringReader) as Activity;
```

we finally build an activity object in the `MenuItem_Click_RunWorkflow` method. Using the following code snippet:

```
WorkflowApplication wfApp = new WorkflowApplication(activity);
wfApp.Run();
```

we run the workflow instance. Please note that as we are running the workflow in a workflows application, there is no need to use `AutoResetEvent` to synchronize threads as we did in console applications.

Implementing visual tracking

In this task, we will create a visual tracking participant. The tracking participant will let the workflow designer display the currently executing activity. When the workflow is executing, the currently executing activity is shown with a yellow outline and debug arrow.

Getting ready

Before we begin this task, we should have completed the previous task: *Implementing XAML Workflow Tab and Run events*.

How to do it...

1. **Open the workflow designer project**:

   Open the workflow designer project we created in the previous task.

2. **Create the VisualTracking participant**:

   Create a new code file named `VisualTracking.cs` and fill the file with the following code:

```
using System;
usingSystem.Collections.Generic;
usingSystem.Activities.Tracking;
usingSystem.Activities.Presentation;
usingSystem.Activities.Presentation.Debug;
usingSystem.Windows.Threading;
usingSystem.Activities.Presentation.Services;
usingSystem.Activities.Debugger;
usingSystem.Activities;
usingSystem.Threading;
namespace WF4Designer {
public class VisualTracking : TrackingParticipant {
privateWorkflowDesignerwd { get; set; }
privateDebuggerServicedebugService { get; set; }
private Dictionary<object, SourceLocation>
sourceLocationMap = null;
//we need a activity id to activity object map
private Dictionary<string, Activity>idActivityMap = null;
publicVisualTracking(WorkflowDesignerwd) {
this.wd = wd;
this.debugService =
wd.DebugManagerView as DebuggerService;
TrackingProfile trackingProfile =
new TrackingProfile();
trackingProfile.Queries.Add(
new ActivityStateQuery {
ActivityName = "*",
States = {
System.Activities.Tracking.
ActivityStates.Executing
},
Variables = { "*" },
Arguments = { "*" }
}
);
this.TrackingProfile = trackingProfile;
sourceLocationMap = GetSourceLocationMap();
idActivityMap = GetIdActivityMap();
}
Dictionary<string, Activity>GetIdActivityMap() {
Dictionary<string, Activity>idToActivity =
new Dictionary<string, Activity>();
foreach (Activity activity in sourceLocationMap.Keys) {
```

```
idToActivity.Add(activity.Id, activity);
}
returnidToActivity;
}
private Activity tempActivity;
protected override void Track(TrackingRecord record,
TimeSpan timeout) {
ActivityStateRecordactivityStateRecord =
record as ActivityStateRecord;
if (activityStateRecord == null)
return;
if (!idActivityMap.ContainsKey(activityStateRecord.
Activity.Id))
return;
wd.View.Dispatcher.Invoke(DispatcherPriority.Render, (Action)(()
=> {
tempActivity = idActivityMap[activityStateRecord. Activity.
Id.ToString()];
wd.DebugManagerView.CurrentLocation = sourceLocationMap[tempActivi
ty];
Thread.Sleep(1000);
}));
}
Dictionary<object, SourceLocation>GetSourceLocationMap() {
Dictionary<object, SourceLocation>runtime_debug =
new Dictionary<object, SourceLocation>();
Dictionary<object, SourceLocation>debug_debug =
new Dictionary<object, SourceLocation>();
System.Activities.Presentation.WorkflowFileItemfileItem =
wd.Context.Items.GetValue(typeof(WorkflowFileItem) )
asWorkflowFileItem;// to get the workflow file path
Activity debugActivity = GetDebugActivity();
Activity runtimeActivity = GetRuntimeActivity();
SourceLocationProvider.CollectMapping(runtimeActivity,
debugActivity,
runtime_debug,
fileItem.LoadedFile);
SourceLocationProvider.CollectMapping(debugActivity,
debugActivity,
debug_debug,
fileItem.LoadedFile);
this.debugService.UpdateSourceLocations(debug_debug);
returnruntime_debug;
}
```

```
        // get activity object from designer
Activity GetDebugActivity() {
ModelServicemodelService =
wd.Context.Services. GetService<ModelService>();
// GetCurrentValue will return ActivityBuilder, actually.
IDebuggableWorkflowTreedebugTree =
modelService.Root. GetCurrentValue()
asIDebuggableWorkflowTree;
if (debugTree != null) {
returndebugTree.GetWorkflowRoot();
} else {
return null;
}
}
// get activity object from the xaml string
Activity GetRuntimeActivity() {// get activity object from the
xaml string
wd.Flush();
System.IO.StringReaderstringReader =
new System. IO.StringReader(wd.Text);
Activity root =
System.Activities.XamlIntegration.
ActivityXamlServices.Load(stringReader);
WorkflowInspectionServices.CacheMetadata(root);
IEnumerator<Activity> list =
WorkflowInspectionServices.GetActivities(root).GetEnumerator();
list.MoveNext();
Activity runtimeActivity = list.Current;
returnruntimeActivity;
}
}
}
```

3. **Add the tracking extension to the workflow designer**:

   Open the designer's backend CS code file and add two code lines to the
   `MenuItem_Click_RunWorkflow` method:

```
private void MenuItem_Click_
RunWorkflow(object sender, RoutedEventArgs e) {
    Save();
    Activity activity = GetActivity();
    WorkflowApplication wfApp = new WorkflowApplication(activity);
    VisualTracking visualTracking = new VisualTracking(wd);
    wfApp.Extensions.Add(visualTracking);
    wfApp.Run();
}
```

4. **Run it**:

   Press *Ctrl+F5* to run the workflow designer; we shall see the following:

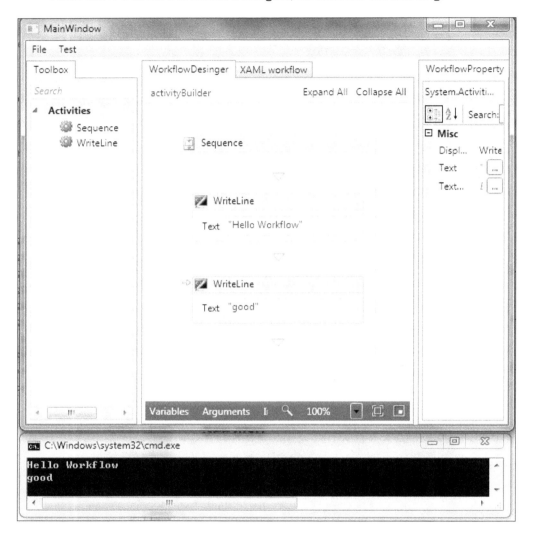

A workflow tree from the workflow runtime doesn't have the source location information, while an `IDebuggableWorkflowTree` tree generated from the designer has the source location information. To highlight the runtime activities in the designer, we can use `SourceLoactionProvider` to extract the source location information from the `IDebuggableWorkflowTree`.

To understand the visual tracking, we need to understand two mappings.

▶ **Activity instance to Activity XAML text location:**

In the source code, we declare a `sourceLocationMap`:

```
private Dictionary<object, SourceLocation>
sourceLocationMap = null;
```

To implement the mapping, we first need to get root activity instance from the designer model service. This activity instance has the source location information.

```
// get activity object from designer
Activity GetDebugActivity() {// get activity object from designer
ModelServicemodelService =
wd.Context.Services. GetService<ModelService>();
// GetCurrentValue will return ActivityBuilder, actually.
IDebuggableWorkflowTreedebugTree =
modelService.Root. GetCurrentValue()
as IDebuggableWorkflowTree;
if (debugTree != null) {
returndebugTree.GetWorkflowRoot();
} else {
return null;
}
}
```

We then need to get a root activity instance from the XAML string. This activity instance will be executed in the workflow runtime; it doesn't have the source location information.

```
// get activity object from the xaml string
Activity GetRuntimeActivity() {// get activity object from the
xaml string
wd.Flush();
System.IO.StringReaderstringReader =
 new System. IO.StringReader(wd.Text);
Activity root =
System.Activities.XamlIntegration.
ActivityXamlServices.Load(stringReader);
WorkflowInspectionServices.CacheMetadata(root);
IEnumerator<Activity> list =
WorkflowInspectionServices.GetActivities(root).GetEnumerator();
list.MoveNext();
Activity runtimeActivity = list.Current;
returnruntimeActivity;
}
```

Now, we need to implement the map:

```
Dictionary<object, SourceLocation> GetSourceLocationMap() {
```

```
Dictionary<object, SourceLocation>runtime_debug =
new Dictionary<object, SourceLocation>();
Dictionary<object, SourceLocation>debug_debug =
new Dictionary<object, SourceLocation>();
// to get the workflow file path
System.Activities.Presentation.WorkflowFileItemfileItem =
wd.Context.Items.GetValue(typeof(WorkflowFileItem)) as
WorkflowFileItem;
Activity debugActivity = GetDebugActivity();
Activity runtimeActivity = GetRuntimeActivity();
SourceLocationProvider.CollectMapping(runtimeActivity,
debugActivity, runtime_debug, fileItem.LoadedFile);
SourceLocationProvider.CollectMapping(debugActivity,
debugActivity,debug_debug,
fileItem.LoadedFile);
this.debugService.UpdateSourceLocations(debug_debug);
returnruntime_debug;
}
```

Let's now analyze the code. Consider the following code statement:

```
SourceLocationProvider.CollectMapping(runtimeActivity,
debugActivity,
runtime_debug,
fileItem.LoadedFile);
```

This statement creates an activity map from workflow runtime to source location so that we can find the source location when the activity is running. Now, we have the source location, but the designer still doesn't know which activity to highlight; so, we need the following code to let the designer be aware of the relation of the source location and the highlighted activities.

```
SourceLocationProvider.CollectMapping(debugActivity,
debugActivity, debug_debug, fileItem.LoadedFile);
```

This statement creates an activity map from designer o source location. And now consider the following code line:

```
this.debugService.UpdateSourceLocations(debug_debug);
```

This line renews the activity to source location map stored in the designer.

▶ **Activity id to activity object:**

In the source code, we declare the following:

```
private Dictionary<string, Activity> idActivityMap = null;
```

Then we map the activity ID to the activity object itself and return a dictionary object that contains the mapping information.

```
Dictionary<string, Activity> GetIdActivityMap() {
```

```
    Dictionary<string, Activity> idToActivity =
        new Dictionary<string, Activity>();
    foreach (Activity activity in sourceLocationMap.Keys) {
        idToActivity.Add(activity.Id, activity);
    }
    return idToActivity;
}
```

Using these two mappings, our visual tracking participant can locate the activity in the designer panel according to its ID:

```
protected override void Track(TrackingRecord record,
TimeSpan timeout) {
ActivityStateRecordactivityStateRecord =
record as ActivityStateRecord;
if (activityStateRecord == null)
return;
if (!idActivityMap.ContainsKey(activityStateRecord.Activity. Id))
return;
wd.View.Dispatcher.Invoke(DispatcherPriority.Render, (
Action) (() => {
tempActivity =
idActivityMap[activityStateRecord.Activity. Id.ToString()];
wd.DebugManagerView.CurrentLocation =
sourceLocationMap[tempActivity];
Thread.Sleep(1000);
}));
}
```

See also

▶ For more information about tracking, one can refer to the *Creating a FileTrackingParticipant* section in *Chapter 6, WF4 Extensions*.

Index

A

abstract Activity class 147, 150
activity
  AddToCollection<T> activity 130
  ClearCollection<T> activity 133
  creating, by inheriting root activity 147
  customizing 148
  ExistsInCollection<T> activity 141
  reference, adding to ActivityLibrary 148
  RemoveFromCollection<T> activity 137
  running 149
  testing, workflow created 148, 149
  working 150
activity designer, for MySquence activity
  creating 170, 171
  designer attribute, adding 171
  running 172
  testing, workflow created 172
  working 173
activity designer, for SendEmail activity
  creating 164-167
  designer attribute, adding to SendMail activity 167, 168
  running 168
  working 169, 170
ActivityLibrary project 146
ActivityXamlServices 34
AddressUri property 100
AddToCollection<T> activity
  about 130
  Console Workflow Application, creating 130
  properties, setting 131
  Sequence activity, dragging to workflow designer 130
  visual workflow, creating 130

  working 132
Appfabric 199
ASP.NET
  workflow service, hosting 206
ASP.NET4 web application, workflow service hosting in ASP.NET
  creating 206
Asynchronous Http Get activity
  creating 159
  running 160, 161
  testing, workflow created 160
  working 161
AsyncHttpGet activity. *See* **Asynchronous Http Get activity**

B

bookmark
  used, for creating Input Message Activity 156
  MyReadLine activity, customizing 25-28

C

CacheMetadata method 198
CancellationScope activity
  code workflow file, creating 108, 110
  using 108
  Workflow Console Application, creating 108
  working 110
CanCreateInstance property 97
C# Code
  Console Application project, creating 9
  reference, adding to System.Activities assembly 9
  used, for creating WF program 9
  workflow definition code, creating 10
  working 10

ClearCollection<T> activity
properties, setting 134, 135
Sequence activity, dragging to workflow designer 134
visual workflow, creating 134
Workflow Console Application, creating 133
working 135
code workflow file, CancellationScope activity
creating 108
CollectionInArg property 128
CollectionPrinter activity 133
CollectionPrinter.cs file 126
**CollectValues, MyPersistenceParticipant
class 194**
compensable activity
host code, creating 121
used, for performing compensation 117
used, for performing manual compensation
120-122
workflow code, creating 118, 120
Workflow Console Application project, creating
118, 120
workflow host code, creating 119
working 119, 122
compensation
performing, Compensable activity used
117-122
composite activity
creating 161
MySquence activity, creating 161-163
running 163, 164
**configuration code, WCF message in code
workflow**
adding 94
confirm activity
used, for performing compensation 122
Workflow Console Application project, creating
123
workflow host code, creating 124
working 124
confirmation
performing, Confirm activity used 122-124
ConpletionCondition property 111
**Console Workflow Application,
AddToCollection<T> activity**
creating 130
Console Workflow Application,

ExistsInCollection<T> activity
creating 141
**Console Workflow Application,
RemoveFromCollection<T> activity**
creating 137
CorrelationScope 108
customized extension
creating 195
host code, creating 196, 197
running 197
workflow, authoring 196
Workflow Console Application, creating 195
working 197

D

database, TransactionScope activity
creating, for testing 112
DataTemplate element 170
**Default.aspx page, workflow service hosting
in ASP.NET**
altering 209, 210
Delay activity 186
designer layout
building 224
empty event handlers, adding 223
implementing 220
running 224
working 224
WPF application project, creating 220, 221
XAML layout code, creating 221, 222
Dictionary<T> object 14
divided-by-zero exception 116
Duration property 184
DynamicActivity 11

E

empty event handlers, designer layout
adding, to behind code file 223
ETW
about 175
running 178
tracking, enabling 177
workflow, authoring 176
Workflow Console Application project, creating
176

workflow host, creating 177, 178

working 179, 180

Event Tracing for Windows. *See* **ETW**

Execute method 150, 153, 163

ExistsInCollection<T> activity

about 141

Console Workflow Application, creating 141

properties, setting 142

Sequence activity, dragging in designer panel 141

workflow, creating 141

working 143

F

FileTrackingParticipant

creating 180

running 182

Tracking Participant 180

workflow, authoring 180

workflow host, creating 181, 182

workflow project, creating 180

working 182

File Writer activity

creating 150, 151

running 152

testing, workflow created 152

working 153

FLOW 41

Flowchart

ReadNumberActivity, creating to guess number 50, 52

workflow project, creating 50

working 52

FlowSwitch<T> activity

workflow, authoring 68, 69

workflow project, creating 67

working 69

Foreach activity

TypeArgument property 45

using 42

UsingForeachActivity namespace, importing to workflow 43

variable, creating 44

Workflow Console Application project, creating 42

working 46

G

GetData activity 103

Grid element 170

Guess number game

in sequence activity 47

ReadNumberActivity, creating to receive guess number 47

workflow, authoring 48

workflow project, creating 47

working 49

Guess number game, Flowchart used

about 49

ReadNumberActivity activity 52

ReadNumberActivity, creating to guess number 50

workflow project, creating 50

working 52

H

HelloWorkflow, WF program

creating 6

Workflow Console Application project, creating 6

workflow program, authoring 7

working 8

host code, compensable activity

creating 121

host code, customized extension

creating 196, 197

I

ICollection<String> type variable 128

ICollection<String> variable 130

IIS7

workflow service, hosting in 200

IIS application, WCF service

creating 82

InArgumentConverter 14

InArguments

Author WF program 12

used, for initializing WF program 11

workflow project, creating 11

working 13, 14

InArgument type 13

InOutArgument
code, writing to host workflow 18
used, for creating WF program 17
workflow, authoring 18
workflow project, creating 17
working 19

Input Message Activity
creating 156
creating, bookmark used 156
running 157
testing, workflow created 156, 157
working 158

InputMessage<T> activity 157

InsertDataToDBActivity code,
TransactionScope activity
creating 113

InvokeMethod activity
using 52
Workflow Console Application, creating 52,
54, 56
workflow project, creating 52
working 57

L

List<T> type Variable 125

load workflow events
code. adding to designer 229, 230
new empty workflow, creating as empty
workflow template 228, 229
workflow designer project, opening 227

M

Main method 152

manual compensation
performing, Compensable activity used 120,
121, 122

MapValues, MyPersistenceParticipant class
194

MenuItem_Click_SaveAs method 235

MenuItem_Click_Save method 234, 235

metadata 163

ModelItems 169

MyPersistenceParticipant class
CollectValues 194
MapValues 194
PublishValues 194

MyReadLine activity
code, writing to host workflow 27, 28
customizing, with bookmark 25, 26
workflow, authorizing 26
workflow project, creating 25
working 28

MySequence activity
activity designer, creating for 170
creating 161

N

NativeActivity. NativeActivity 158

new empty workflow, new workflow events
creating, as an empty workflow template 228,
229

new workflow events
code, adding to designer 229-232
new empty workflow, creating as empty
workflow template 228, 229
workflow designer project, opening 227
working 233

NumberCounter variable 20

O

OutArgument
code, writing to host workflow 16
used, for creating WF program 15
workflow, authoring 15
workflow project, creating 15
working 17

OutMessage 17

P

Parallel activity
workflow, creating 70
workflow project, creating 69
working 71

ParallelForEach<T> activity
using 71
workflow, creating 72, 73
workflow project, creating 71
working 73

persisted workflow
execution sequence 189
loading, from database 185

running 188
workflow, creating 186
workflow host, creating 186, 187
workflow project, creating 186
working 188, 189

persistence database, SQL persistence store
setting up 182-184

persistence participant
custom a CodeActivity 190, 191
persistence participant, creating 190
running 194
using, to persist additional data 189
workflow, creating 191
workflow host, creating 192, 193
workflow project, creating 189
working 194

Pick activity
using 73
workflow, creating 74, 75
workflow host, creating 75
workflow project, creating 73
working 76

print collection items
Workflow Console Application, creating 126, 127
working 129

project
creating 146
WorkflowConsoleApp project 147

project, print collection items
building 127

property inspector view. *See* **workflow designer**

PublishValues, MyPersistenceParticipant class 194

R

Receive activity 87, 97
ReceiveReply activity 108
ReceiveReplyForSend activity 101
ReceiveRequest activity 88
references, TransactionScope activity
adding, to project 113
RemoveFromCollection<T> activity
about 137
Console Workflow Application, creating 137

properties, setting 138
properties setting for 138
workflow, creating 137
working 139

Result property 122
ResumeBookmark method 158
run events
code, adding to designer 236
workflow designer project, opening 236
working 238

S

save as events
code, adding to designer 234, 235
workflow designer project, opening 233
save events
code, adding to designer 234
workflow designer project, opening 233
Save method 234
Secure Sockets Layer. *See* **SSL**
Send activity 97, 102, 107
SendAndReceiveReply activity 100
SendEmail activity
activity designer, creating for 164
creating 153, 154
running 155
testing, workflow created 154
working 155
SendEmailActivity, workflow service hosting in IIS7
adding, to toolbox 200
Send Email workflow service, workflow service hosting in IIS7
creating 201, 202
SendReply activity 87, 92, 97
SendResponse activity 89
Sequence activity 7
service information, WCF message
finding 98, 99
SQL persistence store
configuring 182
persistence database, setting up 182, 184
workflow host, creating 184
workflow project, creating 182
working 185
SQL scripts 182

StartUp project 13
StringReader object 238
svc file, WCF service
  creating 83
Switch<T> activity
  class converter, adding to project 64, 65
  FlowSwitch<T> activity, using 67
  Parallel activity, using 69
  ParallelForEach<T> activity, using 71
  Pick activity, using 73
  test class file Product.cs, creating 64
  using, in Sequence workflow 63
  workflow, authoring 66, 67
  workflow project, creating 63
  working 67
syncEvent 24
syncEvent.Set() 25
System.Activities assembly 9
System.Activities namespace 10
System.Activities.Presentation.ToolboxControl; 220
System.Activities.Presentation.WorkflowDesigner; 219
System.Collection.ObjectModel 127
System.Collections.ObjectModel 127
System.Collections.ObjectModel namespace 134

T

Target property 122
TestMySequenceWF 173
toolbox
  code, adding to designer 224-226
  workflow designer project, opening 224
  working 226, 227
Tracking method 182
transaction
  performing, TransactionScope activity used 112-116
TransactionScope activity
  database, creating for testing 112
  InsertDataToDBActivity code, creating 113
  references, adding to project 113
  used, for performing transaction 112
  workflow code, creating 113
  Workflow Console Application, creating 112

workflow host code, creating 114-116
  working 116
TypeArgument property 45
TypeConverter 14

U

UnitTestForWorkflow 36
unit test framework
  Test Project, adding to solution 34
  unit test code, creating 35, 36
  WF program, testing 34
  workflow file, adding to Test Project 35
  working 36

V

variable
  using, in WF program 20
  workflow, authoring 20
  workflow project, creating 20
  working 22
visual tracking
  creating 238-241
  mappings 243-245
  tracking extension, adding in workflow designer 241
  workflow designer project, opening 238
  working 242
visual workflow, AddToCollection<T> activity
  creating 130
visual workflow, ClearCollection<T> activity
  creating 134
visual workflow, print collection items
  creating 127

W

WCF code, WCF service
  creating 83, 84, 85
WCF message
  receive activity 87
  receiving 98
  sending 98
  SendReply activity 87
  service information, finding out 98, 99
  WCFTestClient, testing in 89, 90

Workflow Console Application project, creating 98
workflow, creating 88, 89, 100-102
workflow project, creating 87
working 91-104

WCF message, in code workflow
code workflow 97
configuration code, adding 94
Receive activity 97, 98
receiving 92, 104
replying 92
Send activity 97, 98
sending 104
visual workflow 97
Workflow Console Application project, creating 92, 104
workflow, creating in code 92-94
workflow, creating in imperative code 104-106
workflow host code, creating 106
WorkflowService class 97
workflow service host code, creating 95
working 97, 107, 108

WCF service
binding 86
contract 86
creating 82
IIS application, creating 82
svc file, creating 83
testing 84, 85
WCF code, creating 83
working 86

WCF (Windows Communication Foundation) 87

WCF workflow service application, workflow service hosting in IIS7
creating 200

WebRequest call 158

WebRequest class 158

website, workflow service hosting in IIS7
creating, in IIS7 204-206

WF4
about 199
error, handling 78
Flowchart workflow 42
FlowSwitch<T> activity 67
Foreach activity 42

Guess number game, in sequence activity 47
InvokeMethod activity 52
Parallel activity 69
ParallelForEach<T> activity 71
Pick activity 73
Sequence workflow 42
Switch<T> activity 63

WF4, activities
AddToCollection<T> activity 130
ClearCollection<T> activity 133
ExistsInCollection<T> activity 141
RemoveFromCollection<T> activity 137

WF4 tracking 179, 180

WF, hosting in Windows Form
about 216
running 218
Windows Form, creating 216, 217, 218
Windows Form project, creating 216
workflow, creating 216
working 218

WF program
code workflow authoring styles, types 6
creating, InOutArgument used 18, 19
debugging 36-38
HelloWorkflow, creating 6-8
instance, converting to XAML 29-31
loading, from XAML file 31-34
prerequisites 6
running, asynchronously 22-25
testing, with unit test framework 34-36
variable used 20-22
variable, using 20
workflow, authoring in XAML 6

WF program, creating
C# Code used 9-11
InOutArgument used 17-19
OutArgument used 15-17

WF program, debugging
debug break point, setting 38
workflow host code, creating 37
workflow project, creating 36

WF program, initializing
InArguments used 11-15

WF program instance
code, writing to create host 29
code, writing to create workflow 29
converting, to XAML 29

workflow project, creating 29
working 31
Windows Form project, WF in Windows Form
creating 216
Windows Form, WF in Windows Form
creating 216, 218
workflow service, hosting 216
WorflowInvoker class 10
**Workflow1.xaml. WorkflowInvoder.Invoke
method 17**
WorkflowApplication class 197
WorkflowApplication object 188
workflow code, compensable activity
creating 118-120
workflow code, TransactionScope activity
creating 113, 114
**Workflow Console Application, Cancellation-
Scope activity**
creating 108
**Workflow Console Application,
ClearCollection<T> activity**
creating 133
**Workflow Console Application, customized
extension**
creating 195, 196
**Workflow Console Application, print collection
items**
creating 126
Workflow Console Application project
compensable activity
compensable activitycreating 120
**Workflow Console Application project, com-
pensable activity**
creating 118
**Workflow Console Application project, confirm
activity**
creating 123
Workflow Console Application project, ETW
creating 176
**Workflow Console Application project, WCF
message**
creating 98
**Workflow Console Application project, WCF
message in code workflow**
creating 92, 104
**Workflow Console Application, Transaction-
Scope activity**

creating 112
WorkflowConsoleApp project 147
workflow, customized extension
authoring 196
workflow designer
code, adding 224-226
workflow designerproject, opening 224
**workflow designer project, new workflow
events**
opening 227
workflow designer project, Run events
opening 236
workflow designer project, Save As events
opening 233
workflow designer project, Save events
opening 233
workflow designer project, visual tracking
opening 238
workflow designer project, XAML workflow tab
opening 236
workflow, ETW
creating 176
workflow, ExistsInCollection<T> activity
creating 141
workflow, FileTrackingParticipant
creating 180
WorkflowForTest.xaml 35
**workflow host code, CancellationScope
activity**
creating 110
workflow host code, compensable activity
creating 119
workflow host code, confirm activity
creating 124
workflow host code, TransactionScope activity
creating 114
**workflow host code, WCF message in code
workflow**
creating 106, 107
workflow host, ETW
creating 177, 178
workflow host, FileTrackingParticipant
creating 181, 182
workflow host, persisted workflow
creating 186, 188
workflow host, persistence participant
creating 192, 193

workflow host, SQL persistence store
creating 184, 185
WorkflowInvoker.Invoke method 11
WorkflowInvoker.Invoker method 25
WorkflowItemsPresenter 173
workflow, persisted workflow
creating 186
workflow, persistence participant
creating 191
workflow project, FileTrackingParticipant
creating 180
workflow project, persisted workflow
creating 186
workflow project, persistence participant
creating 189
workflow project, SQL persistence store
creating 182
workflow project, WCF message
creating 87
workflow, RemoveFromCollection<T> activity
creating 137
WorkflowService class 97
**workflow service host code, WCF message in
    code workflow**
creating 95
workflow service, hosting in ASP.NET
ASP.NET4 web application, creating 206
Default.aspx page, altering 209, 210
running 210
workflow, authoring 206-208
working 211
workflow service, hosting in IIS7
about 200
SendEmailActivity, sending to toolbox
    200, 201
Send Email workflow service, creating
    201, 202
WCF workflow service application, creating
    200
website, creating in IIS7 204-206
working 206
workflow service, hosting in WPF
running 215
workflow, creating 213
working 216
WPF project, creating 213
WPF window, creating 213, 214

workflow, WCF message
creating 88-100
workflow, WCF message in code workflow
creating, in code 92-94
creating, in imperative code 104, 105
workflow, WF in Windows Form
creating 216
workflow, workflow hosting in WPF
creating 213
workflow, workflow service hosting in ASP.NET
authoring 206, 208
WPF
workflow service, hosting 212
WPF application project, designer layout
creating 220, 221
WPF MSDN document
URL 224
WPF project, workflow hosting in WPF
creating 213
WPF window, workflow hosting in WPF
creating 213, 214
WriteLine activity 7, 8, 101

X

XAML
WF program instance, converting to 29
XAML file
code, creating to load up workflow instance
    from XAML string 32, 33
WF program, loading from 31-33
workflow, authoring 32
workflow project, creating 31
working 33, 34
XAML layout code, designer layout
creating 221-223
XamlServices 31
XAML workflow tab
code, adding to designer 236
running 237
workflow designer project, opening 236
working 238

Thank you for buying
Microsoft Windows Workflow Foundation 4.0 Cookbook

About Packt Publishing

Packt, pronounced 'packed', published its first book "*Mastering phpMyAdmin for Effective MySQL Management*" in April 2004 and subsequently continued to specialize in publishing highly focused books on specific technologies and solutions.

Our books and publications share the experiences of your fellow IT professionals in adapting and customizing today's systems, applications, and frameworks. Our solution-based books give you the knowledge and power to customize the software and technologies you're using to get the job done. Packt books are more specific and less general than the IT books you have seen in the past. Our unique business model allows us to bring you more focused information, giving you more of what you need to know, and less of what you don't.

Packt is a modern, yet unique publishing company, which focuses on producing quality, cutting-edge books for communities of developers, administrators, and newbies alike. For more information, please visit our website: www.PacktPub.com.

About Packt Enterprise

In 2010, Packt launched two new brands, Packt Enterprise and Packt Open Source, in order to continue its focus on specialization. This book is part of the Packt Enterprise brand, home to books published on enterprise software – software created by major vendors, including (but not limited to) IBM, Microsoft and Oracle, often for use in other corporations. Its titles will offer information relevant to a range of users of this software, including administrators, developers, architects, and end users.

Writing for Packt

We welcome all inquiries from people who are interested in authoring. Book proposals should be sent to author@packtpub.com. If your book idea is still at an early stage and you would like to discuss it first before writing a formal book proposal, contact us; one of our commissioning editors will get in touch with you.

We're not just looking for published authors; if you have strong technical skills but no writing experience, our experienced editors can help you develop a writing career, or simply get some additional reward for your expertise.

PUBLISHING

Programming Windows Workflow Foundation: Practical WF Techniques and Examples using XAML and C#

ISBN: 978-1-904811-21-3   Paperback: 252 pages

A C# developer's guide to the features and programming interfaces of Windows Workflow Foundation

1. Add event-driven workflow capabilities to your .NET applications.

2. Highlights the libraries, services and internals programmers need to know

3. Builds a practical "bug reporting" workflow solution example app

WCF Multi-tier Services Development with LINQ

ISBN: 978-1-847196-62-0   Paperback: 384 pages

Build SOA applications on the Microsoft platform in this hands-on guide

1. Master WCF and LINQ concepts by completing practical examples and apply them to your real-world assignments

2. First book to combine WCF and LINQ in a multi-tier real-world WCF service

3. Ideal for beginners who want to build scalable, powerful, easy-to-maintain WCF services

Please check **www.PacktPub.com** for information on our titles

www.ingramcontent.com/pod-product-compliance
Lightning Source LLC
LaVergne TN
LVHW062310060326
832902LV00013B/2141